A Tapestry to Tell

poems 1501 – 2000

by

T.P. Russell

1501.
There are those magic moments
When things seem to align;
One minute you are in distress,
The next you're feeling fine.

One day you're torn by torments,
The next you're bathed in joy,
For what's ahead can curse or bless;
Can nurture or destroy.

But here, within the moment,
If you would still your mind,
And take the time to rearrange
You're feelings, you would find

That you've a chance to foment,
In your reality,
A real and everlasting change
To calm that surging sea.

1502.
Welcome Spring, my gentle friend,
Let's raise a glass to Winter's end,
And celebrate the changing of the guard,

Then tell me tales of what's to be,
When nudging nature lovingly
Awake, and I'll tell others as your bard.

1503.
I've watched for the awakening
And now it has begun,
As bursting forth and blossoming
And seeking for the sun,

First here and there, then everywhere
Life breaks through winter's ground
As spring arrives to warm the air
And bid buds be unbound.

1504.
Can you feel it on your skin,
That long-forgotten sun?
Can you feel the growth begin,
That has but just begun?

Can you hear it in your heart,
That song of spring unsprung,
That, sweetly, from the very start,
Has every year been sung?

1505.
All you were and all you'll be
Are tied in continuity
By one small strand that's yours and yours alone,

That, slow and steady, winds and weaves,
Creating patterns you perceive
Upon the cloth from which your soul is sewn.

1506.
With the sun on my face on this cool March morn,
The sparkle of dew draws me in,
To whisper of wonders, all yet to be born,
And thus does a new day begin.

1507.
If nothing else, in life, be kind,

From there all goodness springs,
And from the lack of which you'll find
The darkness evil brings,

For kindness is the root of all
That blossoms beautifully,
And sprouts out of a seed so small,
Yet grows abundantly.

1508.
Oh come, oh come, cool rains of spring,
To you and you alone I sing,
As I stand wet and filled with joyful song,

And praise you for the gift you bring
Of showers on the wakening
Of life, that it grows vigorous and strong.

1509.
In the middle of the night,
When all is still and stars are bright,
I pause and ponder for a bit
If there could be a point to it,

And what I find is not concrete,
Is not a chain of thought complete,
But is assurance there is more
Than I was ever hoping for.

1510.
Green is the color I'm drawn to,
Green and the blue of the sky,
And spring is when clear colors show through
The last days of winter gone by,

For spring is the time of renewal,
So bright and so fresh and so clean,
Of all of the seasons, a jewel;
A glittering garnet of green.

1511.
From the bounty love bestows,
A gift of boundless beauty grows,
That touches all and everything
With everlasting light,

For though there's darkness everywhere,
And evil strikes without a care,
There's power in the love we bring
To set the world aright.

1512.
May I climb up and join you,
Up in those branches high,
And share the wonder you have found
Up there amid the sky?

For when I look upon you,
I see a sparkle there,
That tells me you're no longer bound,
But breathe a better air.

1513.
It's been a long gestation,
From birth through all I've been,
But now I'm ready and await
To be reborn again,

Into a new vocation,

A calling, if you will,
To lose myself, then recreate
Myself from what I kill.

1514.
There will be a blooming soon
From all that has awoken,
As flowers show their beauty everywhere,

And turn their faces, all in tune,
To see from where is spoken
The call to dance amid the April air.

1515.
I remember when we met;
How we were much too young, and yet
We married and had children right away.

I remember how they grew,
And how the love I had for you
Grew deep and rich and stronger every day.

And here we are now, you and I;
So many years have passed us by,
And yet I feel we've only just begun,

For though we're old, we're young at heart
And grown too close to come apart,
But will forever live our lives as one.

1516.
From where does beauty emanate;
From where does joy arise?
How is it some find wonderment

Beneath clear April skies,

While others find no beauty there
Beneath the same clear blue;
Find ugliness and deep despair
No matter what they do?

1517.
We were made for love and light,
What isn't, isn't ours,
For we are beacons burning bright
With never ending fires,

That drive the demons from the night
And light the way to dawn,
Where all will see with perfect sight
The path they're put upon.

1518.
It's there, right there, within your heart
That seeds of honest change must start,
If you desire to see them grow to good.

For it is in your heart alone
That what you're seeking must be sown,
If it's to grow to what you know it could.

1519.
I sit in the woods, as still as can be,
And wait for its magic to come over me,
Then pause in its peace, and doing so see
That I and the woods are as one.

For there is a thread that weaves its way through

This world that we see and these things that we do,
That's pulled by a hand that is steady and true,
From which the world's fabric is spun.

1520.
The earth has seen catastrophe,
But never from her own;
Seen life diminished terribly at times,

But here we are, and hungrily
We've picked her to the bone,
To feed to our consumer paradigm.

1521.
I dreamed last night that I returned
To where I used to play;
The place I lived, where I have yearned
To go again one day,

My parents both were there, alive,
My brother, dead, there too,
But then I felt the day arrive
And woke to what was true.

1522.
There's a place where you'll feel free,
Where you will jump for joy,
And run through meadows happily,
Again a girl or boy,

Without a worry or a care,
Just living day to day,
So turn and seek it if you dare
Before it slips away.

1523.
The child I was lives on within,
I hear that little voice,
I feel that urge to play and make believe.

Still there where it has always been,
And I have made the choice
To love that child so it will never leave.

1524.
The crows played on the wind today
The way I think I might
If I had wings and I could sing
Their song of cawed delight.

Wings are a waste, some people say,
On birds, who do not feel,
But in the way they flew today
I knew their joy was real.

1525.
I walk through the woods as they're coming alive,
And see everywhere the strong will to survive,
As everywhere living things struggle and strive
To burst from the cold earth and sing.

It gives me great hope that the things that we do,
Won't keep life from blooming out each year anew,
And that when we've passed there will still be a few
Small flowers to bloom in the spring.

1526.
I don't care what you do,
It means nothing to me,

Just as long as you're caring and kind,

But what I think of you
Is my own, for I'm free
To believe what I will with my mind.

1527.
Be awake and aware
That you're living out there
In the world, and deep down in your head,

For the mix of the two
At the border is you,
Where all conscious awareness is bred.

1528.
Everywhere I look I see
The features of fecundity
Alerting and reminding me
That we are not alone;

That nature moves incessantly
Toward some end we cannot see,
That we can culture carefully,
But we can never own.

1529.
They come upon us in a flash,
Then quickly fall away,
Those memories, so rich and real,
Each of some yesterday,

Then pass perception in a dash,
To where, we cannot say,

But wake us up and make us feel
The way we did one day.

1530.
Look out as though this were the first
You've looked upon the world;
Look out and leave what holds you back behind,

For out of what appeared the worst,
Today you have been hurled,
Into the now to see what you might find.

1531.
Look around and you will see
An infinite variety
Of shapes and forms and sizes
In this world of constant change,

And change, not stasis, forms the core
Of all these things you're seeing, for
Reality arises
As they shift and rearrange.

1532.
These cool, wet woods are dotted
With spatterings of white,
As all the dogwoods bloom as one
And cast a living light,

Whose rays are tightly knotted
Into this tapestry
That I have only just begun
To see coherently.

1533.
Today I saw a rainbow,
Lit by the setting sun,
While I stood in the rain until it passed.

Two arcs about a shadow,
Their light so soon was done,
Like all in life that fades away so fast.

1534.
On the one hand there's the brain,
That struggles so against the strain
We have to find a quiet place and rest,

While on the other there's the soul
That seeks, in silence, to be whole
And knows that it's in emptiness we're blessed.

1535.
I love the sound of water
A-runnin in a stream;
I love the way it carries me
Into a gentle dream,

Where nothing seems to matter
And everything is good,
For when I'm there and floating free
All seems the way it should.

1536.
Get out of your head and look all around,
And you'll be amazed at the fun to be found,
Just take in each color, each shape and each sound,
And make them your life and your love.

For out in the world you'll find all that is real,
And I am not saying don't think and don't feel,
But that there is much looking out can reveal
That you are incognizant of.

1537.
Until the day it darkens
I'll shine my light on you,
Until there's no more life inside
I'll try to live it true.

Until the day it hearkens
To leave the flesh behind,
My soul will journey by your side
And mingle with your mind.

1538.
Like a weed in a crack
When you're flat on your back,
Push up through the weight of oppression,

And rise up happily,
From your bonds and be free,
To bloom in the light of elation.

For the strength that you seek,
When you're weary and weak,
Will come out of the power within,

Whose limits are none,
And that shines like the sun,
So gather your strength and begin.

1539.
We all began as wild things,
Who met the world with rage,
When wrestled from the womb so wet and warm,

But living in this world brings
The need to pay the wage
Of taking on a false and foreign form,

And in that transformation,
Our spirits were repressed,
To such a point we hardly know the child,

But if we seek cessation
Of wants we will be blessed
With finding once again that we are wild.

1540.
In the dull rain there's a glimmer
Of morning light dancing in dew,
That shone ere the daylight grew dimmer
And darkened its heavenly view.

When all appears dull, dead and dreary;
When nothing seems livened with light,
Awaken, though you have grown weary,
And seek out that spark in the night.

1541.
You taught me love and laughter,
You taught me to be kind,
You showed me all, in this whole world,
I'll ever need to find.

Before we met, and after,

Are separate lives I've led;
The latter like a flag unfurled
The moment we were wed.

1542.
The self is a shell that your living maintains,
That formed when your life came to be,
And held in its form by societal chains,
It won't let your spirit break free,

But deep down within there's a sonorous sound
As the spirit sings steady and true,
So break from your bonds till your whole self is bound
To the magic that lives within you.

1543.
You're living in a fiction
Defining who you are,
Whose draft was writ before you came to be,

Then given depth and diction,
That marked you like a scar,
When you were forced to follow faithfully.

But you're the author of it;
Your edits are your own,
And you can scrap the ending if you choose,

And twist the plot within it
To say what you condone,
And make of it the markings of the muse.

1544.
You are what you are, not what others assign;

You are who you've been from the start,
So live that the self and the spirit align,
And center your life on your heart.

1545.
The sound of rain and birdsong
Awoke me from my sleep,
Out of that place of emptiness,
So still and dark and deep,

And though I've lived here so long,
The world each day is new,
Where all exudes a happiness
At waking fresh and true.

1546.
Can you feel the spirit?
It pulls me (does it you?),
Away from what I'm striving toward
And where I'm heading to,

To come and live within it,
As it lives deep in me,
And live my life in full accord
With true transcendency.

1547.
There's life in every drop of dew,
Too small for you to see,
Just as all in and out of you,
And in and out of me,

There lives a mighty multitude
That calls your body home;

Most help you live, but some have chewed
Into your tattered tome.

And all those pages tell a tale
Of struggle to survive;
Of fighting those that make us fail,
And keeping those alive

That seek that symbiotic state
Of helping out the host
Stay healthy and rejuvenate,
Till giving up the ghost.

1548.
You miss the playfulness you had
When you were very young,
You miss the carefree days of endless play,

But there's a lassie or a lad
Who sings the song you sung,
And waits within to sing again one day.

1549.
I watched a 'possum rot away
Along the path I walk each day,
Just melt and merge into the clay
Until it was no more.

From lifeless matter we arise,
To bloom beneath clear summer skies,
But all that lives here lives and dies.
What are you living for?

To gather things up as your own?
Is that the calling you condone?

To find the future you've been shown
Of having more and more?

Have all your treasures brought you peace
And made your lustful longings cease?
Will you be ready for release
When death knocks at your door?

1550.
The way the sunlight sparkles,
And dances on the dew,
Reminds me of the way I feel
When I encounter you,

As I awake each morning
And look upon your face,
And see you looking back at me,
With eyes the gift of grace.

1551.
What have they done
With that bright summer sun,
That used to shine forth from your face?

Is it still shining there
Behind clouds of despair?
I look, but I don't see a trace

Of the light I once knew;
Is it still inside you?
I pray it shines out from within,

When the heat of your heart
Makes the clouds break apart,
So you can see blue skies again.

1552.
I have a voice,
It is my own,
I'll use it my own way,

For I've the choice
To set the tone
Of what I choose to say.

And what you say,
Well that's your own
And isn't up to me,

But you'll not sway
Me to condone
If I do not agree.

1553.
There's a window in the wall,
Out of which you can see,
The perfect presence of it all
In crystal clarity,

And yet you're fully focused on
The paintings you have hung,
Depicting deeds that you have done
And dreams your soul has sung,

And maybe you are happy there
With how they make you feel,
But for one moment, shift your stare
And gaze at what is real.

1554.
"Well goodness gracious sakes alive",

That's what she used to say, and I've
Still got my mother's words here in my head.

I treasure, very deeply, all
I hear now as colloquial;
I miss her way with words no longer said.

1555.
What is it that you'll do today
To set the world on fire;
What mountains must you move to make a start?

It need not be a grand display,
For all that you'll require
Is to emit a movement from the heart.

1556.
Look at the world with the eyes of a child,
Who sees everything fresh and new,
For over the years, we've all been beguiled
By living the way that we do,

We've all been beguiled by thinking somehow
Things are what we think them to be,
But the truth of it all is we only know now
The edges of reality.

1557.
Are you a boiling pot of pure emotion,
That threatens every day to overflow?
If so, turn down the heat and know the notion
That things are better when they simmer slow.

1558.

Ignite the fire of pure imagination
And cast its light on what you think is real,
Then ponder with unconscious contemplation,
This life, in which you think and breathe and feel.

This life, that has been formed to fit the notion
That you'd be best to follow faithfully,
But if you'd only move to your own motion,
You'd find the happiness you seek to see.

1559.

Let's all try our best to be
Aware of one another,
And treat each other lovingly
As sister or as brother,

And celebrate that each is free
To sing with their own song,
While knowing when we don't agree
We need not sing along.

1560.

The geese are flying overhead,
I hear their distant call,
As they pass north to where they'll raise their young.

I'll hear them later in my bed,
Remembering last fall,
When last I heard the traveling song they sung.

1561.

Seek joy in everything you do,
And spread that joy to others who

Might not be finding what it is you've found,

For all the joy you're finding there
Is there to gather up and share;
Is there for each of us to spread around.

1562.
When you end your final day,
And self awareness slips away,
Will you be happy with the way
You lived the life you led?

With what you did this very day?
With what you chose to do and say?
Or find you wasted time away
Now that you're nearly dead?

1563.
Just watch, sometime, a child at play;
Watch how they while away the day,
Pursuing pointless pleasures
With a pure and perfect peace.

When did we trade simplicity
For uncontrolled complexity?
When did we trade our treasures
For a hunger that won't cease?

1564.
Joy and sorrow come to be
As fruits upon a single tree
Whose roots have reached down deep into your soul,

One comes from yearnings not attained,

The other from the same, when gained,
And tasting of the two makes life a whole.

1565.
Open like a flower in the morning,
That shows itself amid the drying dew;
Open wide to satisfy the yearning,
To share the love that others share with you.

Open wide and live a life worth living,
And shine your light on everyone you see;
Shine that they might flourish in your giving,
And you will find you flourish equally.

1566.
Don't pursue a path of pure appeasement
With enemies, that they be satisfied,
Seek instead the way of true fulfillment,
And walk with those who love you at your side.

Nothing's gained by pleasing those who harm you,
Though doing so might make them leave you be,
Turn instead and seek a path that seems true,
And walk out of the rut of rivalry.

1567.
What's hurting you may pass away
Like other woes that came your way,
To mingle with the memories
You made down in the mire,

But bear the ones that choose to stay,
And pull yourself out of dismay,
By seeking possibilities

To raise your spirits higher.

1568.
As I near the finish line
I wonder what I'll win.
When I end this life of mine
Will something new begin?

Will I be rewarded for
The race I chose to run,
Or when at last there is no more
Will sense of self be done?

1569.
A tiny rill is running,
A trickle like a tear,
That flows across slick, mossy stone
So quiet, cool and clear.

I feel here a beginning,
A starting out anew,
With youthful eyes, though I am grown,
That seek to see what's true.

1570.
If you were to pass away
What would my compass be,
For you have always acted as my guide?

I ask, then ask, what guides your day
That should be guiding me,
If I no longer had you by my side?

1571.
Know your heart
And know it well,
Be who it is you are,

Don't play the part
They try to sell,
For you're a shining star.

Yes, you're a star
That's burning bright
To grace the evening sky,

And you'll burn far
Into the night
Before the day you die.

1572.
This body that you're born in
Is yours and yours alone,
No one can tell you what to do or say,

And when that rule you've broken,
You surely can atone
By letting others live in their own way.

1573.
Your world is awash with wonder,
But wonderment wells from within,
And you're either in it or under
A cloud of unspeakable sin,

The sin of just focusing inward
And missing the things that are real,
The sin of not focusing forward;

The falling of failing to feel.

1574.
When happiness depends upon
Things out of your control,
You're bound to have a bad day now and then,

But you can choose to base life on
The singing of the soul,
For happiness wells always from within.

1575.
To see it all through limpid eyes,
To see it bright and bare,
You must remove the dark disguise
The world has made you wear,

That mask that all gets filtered through
To alter and conceal,
So shed the shield that shelters you
And look at what is real.

1576.
Stop a moment, listen
To what's not in your head,
And quell the constant chatter for a while,

Then let the quiet christen
Your soul, that's nearly dead
To what is real; in silence sit and smile.

1577.
Inside there's an ocean of stillness,

A sea of unquenchable calm,
Whose waters are waiting to soothe you
And be as your balancing balm,

To empty, then fill you with fullness,
And drift you through dreams of delight,
Composed of the memories that move you,
That come and go all through the night.

1578.
Life's like a river that constantly flows,
Gathering volume the further it goes,
Ending up where no one living here knows;
To maybe end up in a sea,

You are the steersman determining where
You'll paddle your boat, or float without care,
Picking a path that your body will bear
Through currents that pull endlessly.

1579.
I hunger for simplicity
And find it everyday,
For it lies at the very root of all,

Where covered by complexity
It's always hid away
To find behind the world's unwieldy wall.

1580.
On the one hand are the things
We treat as tried and true,
On the other are the things
We question through and through,

But when we label things as true
We rarely reassess,
Lest we find fractures when we do
That halt our happiness.

1581.
It is the hungry and the poor
That we should all be praying for;
It is the hopeless and the dispossessed,

Who know that they will never know
The fullness and the happy glow
Of those they see, who have from birth been blessed.

1582.
I watch as they pose,
Pretending to be
The things that they know they are not,

How is it they chose
To live like I see,
What drove them to get where they got?

1583.
My body says yes but my spirit says no,
There's simply no telling which way it will go,
I hope in the end that my choices will show
A life lived with others in mind.

And all I can do is make one at a time,
One choice of my choosing, for in the end I'm
An author that authors my own paradigm;
I hope mine is caring and kind.

1584.
Adrift amid the choppy sea
Of endless possibility
You fight the waves that come and go
While losing sight of land,

For when you flail and thrash around
You're drawn away from solid ground,
But if you float and trust the flow
You'll wash up on the sand.

1585.
Life's a long, slow march toward
The precipice you fear,
Or it's a stroll through grassy meadows bright,

But either way the common chord
Is that the end draws near
With every step, so take each with delight.

1586.
Within a thing most simple,
Complexity abounds,
For nothing is as simple as it seems,

Like life, which in its dimple
Of space-time has no bounds,
For vast are the dimensions of our dreams.

1587.
If the veil were parted,
Allowing you to see,
For just a moment, undisguised,
The full reality,

That's been so closely guarded,
And masked so carefully,
You'd very likely be surprised
By its simplicity.

1588.
Your life, it is a beautiful equation,
That answers all your questions all along.
"What is", you ask, "the point of each occasion?",
"What is", says life, "a note within a song?"

1589.
Seek always the mysterious,
Search for the ways unknown;
You'll find it lying right before your eyes,

For just a peek is shown to us,
Like skin that hides the bone,
But so much more is there to realize.

1590.
No matter where you're going
I want to ride along,
No matter what we're singing
It's gonna be our song,

We'll pick a road at random
And ride it to the end;
We'll ride with wild abandon,
For baby, you're my friend.

Yea baby you're what moves me,
What stills me when I'm wild,
You loose the ties that bind me

To free my inner child,

To jump with jubilation
And run this road we ride,
Where we'll find affirmation,
Each with the perfect guide.

And when the road gets rougher,
We'll take it all in stride,
For we'll find we've grown tougher
While by each other's side,

And when the sun sets brightly
As we approach the end,
We'll hold each other tightly,
For baby, you're my friend.

1591.
Listen to the music of the ages,
That plays upon the gentle morning breeze,
For in it is the knowledge of the sages;
A wealth of wisdom for your soul to seize.

Hearken to the melody of morning,
As you walk barefoot through the damp of dew,
Each diamond dot a diadem adorning
A blade of grass that sings its song for you,

Take it in and take it where it leads you,
Take it in and let the journey start,
And you will find the place the lyrics lead to,
Will be the very center of your heart.

1592.
You were not made to stand alone,

You couldn't if you tried;
There's sadness in a solitary soul,

That yearns to know and to be known;
To share the life inside,
With others, that in others it be whole.

1593.
I stood and watched a flower,
And watched a tiny bee,
And came to the conclusion
They're no different from me,

And in that endless hour,
(Or was it very brief?),
While lost in an illusion,
I expanded my belief.

1594.
What is it you worship that sustains you?
What nourishes your body and your soul?
Peace and love should be what it pertains to;
To foster peace and love should be your goal.

That is all there is worth holding onto,
And nothing else will feed your hungry heart
Like releasing everything you cling to,
So shed the selfish self and make a start.

1595.
Each day, awake and born anew,
Discover something wholly new
That you have never known
In all the days you lived before,

For there is an infinity
Of wonders waiting patiently,
That one day will be shown
If you but always look for more.

1596.
There it is, I've found it,
That thing I sought so long,
I'd circled all around it
But where I'd looked was wrong,

For it was never hidden
But, bathed in brilliant light,
Revealed itself when bidden
As always in plain sight.

1597.
When you're adrift out in the sea
Of endless possibility
Let me row out and offer you a hand,

And here's the lifeline I will throw,
Stop thinking that you'll ever know
Which course is best, just row and pray for land.

1598.
If you would but abandon all desire,
You'd see beyond these objects that you see;
You'd see they're but reflections from the fire
That feeds upon the true reality.

These images are all you'll ever know,
But in their shifting shadows they reveal,
In bits and pieces as they come and go,

The truth behind the things you think are real.

1599.
Nothing here exists in isolation,
But only in relation to the rest,
As properties, formed from the interaction
Of entities, as matter, manifest,

To take their final form when observation
Occurs between the separate entities,
And thus create, between the two, relations
As one of infinite realities.

And that's the base of being at the bottom,
But at a scale too small for us to see.
For things for us don't jump about at random,
But stay their course with solid certainty.

Knowing that, though, gives a sense of wonder,
That though there's no foundation down below;
No solid base of matter lying under
This world of solid substance that we know,

We still can understand, through observation,
These things in nature that the senses feel,
And knowing that they stand on no foundation,
Perceive them still as meaningful and real.

1600.
Without a place of darkness
Your light would never show,
Without the gnaw of emptiness
You'd never come to know

The feel, when found, of fullness,

Of basking in its glow,
For out of longing happiness
Will, like a garden, grow.

1601.
I cannot help but to believe
There's more than what the eyes perceive;
That we see just the surface
Of a world that has no end,

That we are each a tongue of fire
That's fed from an eternal pyre;
That we each don a nimbus;
To great heights we'll each ascend.

1602.
Look, it is vertiginous,
It's bound to blow your mind,
These depths that lie in each of us,
These chasms unconfined,

These inner lives, mysterious,
Where you will surely find,
A love, so grand and glorious,
With your heart, intertwined.

1603.
We only know a little bit
About what's going on,
'Though we are learning more and more each day.

Just half awake and sleepy-eyed
We've stepped into the dawn,
And think we know enough to find our way.

But there is little that we know
And less we understand,
Though we have mastered all we've set to learn.

Yet there is always room to grow
As we walk hand-in-hand,
And mysteries to find at every turn.

1604.
Tell me do they move you,
These words you write and read,
Or do they pass right through you
And never plant a seed,

That grows into a garden,
A paradise of thought,
Where no one thing can harden;
Where preference plays no plot?

1605.
Tell me of your ethics,
Pray tell, what do they say,
Do they extend beyond what you
Are living every day?

Do they include the basics
Of caring for the land?
Do they reflect a heart that's true;
Define a selfless stand?

1606.
Loss and grief are never brief
But linger on forever,
To test and challenge your belief

That time will one day sever

The pain and sorrow of your loss
From what you know each day,
But in the end the pain of loss
Will fade, but not away.

1607.
We project upon the world what we expect to see,
And reassess the world a bit with each discrepancy,
And so erect a model made out of consistency;
A model that we call reality.

But it is just a model that we form from what we find,
A course interpretation of what's real held in the mind,
So we must work to stay outside and not get trapped behind
These walls we raise, for they can make us blind.

1608.
It is in total emptiness
That fullness can be found;
A fullness that encompasses it all,

That leads to total happiness;
A burst of bliss unbound,
When you let all the things you've gathered fall.

1609.
The path to true tranquility,
Will show itself at times to me,
As there, in crystal clarity
To set my feet upon,

But when I've walk a little way,

It seems I'm always turned away,
By some distracting disarray,
And then the path is gone.

1610.
Listen, is it speaking?
What does it have to say?
The answers you are seeking
Are found no other way,

Than heightening awareness
And taking always in,
And listening with eagerness
To what has always been.

1611.
In the silence of your mind
Is where awareness waits,
To soak in what your senses find
And what your brain creates,

And make, from that which you take in,
A model of the real,
That's built from all that's ever been
Impressed on what you feel.

1612.
The world is well defined and we
Believe we know it thoroughly,
But there is very little that we know,

For all we know is what we see,
These shadows of reality,
These fleeting hints of truth that come and go.

1613.
The world is not of matter made,
Though it appears to be
Much more than just a shifting shade
Of possibility,

But that is what, down deep below,
Defines reality,
For it's been found things do not grow
From seeds of certainty.

1614.
Though all seems made of matter,
That's not what we perceive,
It's only the relations that we know.

And what creates the latter?
In what can we believe?
In these I say, these solid shapes that show.

1615.
These sounds of summer take me back
To when I was a child;
To sultry summer evenings long ago,

When days were long and nights were black,
And all the world was wild,
And time, that now moves fast, slipped by so slow.

1616.
At the root of everything
There's nothing much at all;
No solid base to build belief upon,

No firmament on which to cling,
For at the very small,
All semblance of certainty is gone.

1617.
I walk along forgotten fields,
Long left and overgrown,
Recovering from years of yields
From seeds that had been sown,

And marvel at how quick it goes
Back as it used to be;
How order from the hand that sows
Disperses rapidly.

1618.
Can you feel it flowing,
Just like a gentle stream,
That always has been going
Towards a distant dream;

That moves you ever onward,
And carries you away,
As it flows ever forward
To meet a better day?

1619.
Love is like two mountain streams
Whose waters join as one;
Like dreamers tangled in a dream
That cannot be undone.

For love is patient and will wait,
But when two hearts combine,

The brilliant light the two create
Forevermore will shine.

1620.
What is the You you know so well?
How did it come to be,
From birth to death, a single cell
Of continuity?

For you're a single, changeless thread
Of subjectivity;
The same, forever, in your head
Self conscious entity.

1621.
What will the world be without you?
Will it be any less when you die?
Does goodness spring forth from what you do?
Are you selfless; do you even try

To give of yourself every moment,
And take only that which you need?
Or does your self-centeredness foment
A world that is growing in greed?

1622.
I've read that form is emptiness
And emptiness is form,
And feel, deep in my heart it could be true,

But to believe with earnestness
What goes against the norm
To that extent is very hard to do.

1623.
I feel it move within me,
A birthing, if you will,
A welling up of wonder from within,

To paint the world around me,
And doing so distill
The essence of the now from all that's been.

1624.
I truly hope to walk one day
Along the narrow middle way;
That line where all that was meets what's to be,

For though I cross it now and then,
The what's to be and what has been
Is where, it seems, I walk exclusively.

1625.
When you were young you never talked
About the life you led,
But eager for what's new you walked
On virgin paths instead,

But now you only reminisce
About that younger you,
And doing so you often miss
What's interesting and new.

1626.
How deeply are you rooted?
Are you on fertile land,
Or do you cling to dry and rocky ground?

Do you feel you're not suited
For where it is you stand,
And think it's time to bolt from where you're bound?

If so, think how you got there,
And what it is you've done
To make that place a better place to be,

For what you seek is somewhere,
And this could be the one
True paradise if you'd but look and see.

1627.
Is there a constant cycle of existence?
Is there a place we go to when we're gone?
Or is it wishful thinking, this insistence
That when we die we somehow carry on?

Of course we'll never know until we get there;
Until we slip into that mystery,
But while we're on our way these lives that we share
Are all we have that sings of certainty.

1628.
Many, many years ago
When still my world was young,
I sang the first few verses of
This song that I have sung,

And I'll continue till there's no
More words to fill the page
For I have found this song I love
Has bettered me with age.

1629.
When life first stirred within you
You woke to who you are,
And still remain the same as you were then,

And will until it leaves you,
That solitary star,
That seed of self that you have always been.

But what of the beginning?
And what about the end?
Were you before? Will you be after death?

It sets my head to spinning
To think we might extend
As self beyond the first and final breath.

1630.
This moment's really all you've got,
The rest are what has been,
And all those yet to come may not,
So live the one you're in.

1631.
I think I've nearly found the peace
That I have long desired,
For I have hoped this search would cease
Before I'm old and tired,

And what, you ask, is it I found
That brought about such bliss?
It's nothing but to be unbound
And echo emptiness.

1632.
Try your best to be unbound
And echo emptiness,
For in unfettered freedom's found
The heart of happiness.

1633.
I watched the clouds drift by today,
And as the day went by,
They changed from white to red to gray,
Then blackened with the sky,

And stars blinked out as they passed by
To show where they might be,
As blobs of blackness in the sky
That slid by silently.

1634.
It is in total emptiness
That fullness can be found,
For when you learn to live with less
You'll be no longer bound

To things that bring you anxiousness,
And when you've let them go,
You'll find the perfect peacefulness
You thought you'd never know.

1635.
Our understanding's incomplete,
There's nothing that we know,
That isn't soon made obsolete
By finer facts that show,

For though we hone the things we know
Down to a razor edge,
On closer look that line does show
To be a jagged ledge.

1636.
Oh the gentle morning song
The waking world does sing,
To it I rise and sing along;
What joy the voices bring.

They center me and help me find,
Anew, at break of day,
A path on which to set my mind;
A sign to show the way.

1637.
All there really is to know
Is life's a mystery;
That nothing can be known, although
We try wholeheartedly

To understand, and have success
In much of what we do,
But nothing's fully known unless
We know it through and through.

1638.
My angel took my hand when I
Was drifting aimlessly,
To set me on a course we two could share,

And as our years have passed us by,
I've slowly come to see

That I'd be lost but for my angel's care.

For I've a wild and reckless side
That's never served me well,
And would have ruined me had we two not met,

But with my angel as my guide,
And our paths parallel,
I've lived a life I know I'll not regret.

1639.
This life I live does surely seem
To be, to me, a drifting dream,
From which, one day, with wonder, I'll awake,

But what it is I'll wake to find
Is not a thing this simple mind
Can know, for all seems partial and opaque.

1640.
Stop to look around you
And you might realize
That what you're really looking for
Is right before your eyes;

Is all laid out before you,
As it has always been,
And you will never want for more,
If you'd but take it in.

1641.
It is, in life, those little things
That makes a life worth living;
Those little blooms that blossom so inside,

Whose burst of budding beauty brings
A bounty bound for giving
To those who tend this garden at your side.

1642.
This beauty I'm beholding
Is constantly unfolding,
And opens like a flower in the spring,

That cannot help but growing,
Fed by the inner knowing
That life's a song we all together sing.

1643.
There's a little voice inside
That tells me what to do,
And steers me as a steady guide
To take trails tried and true,

But there's another voice within
(Or is it from without?)
That calls to me when I begin
To stray away in doubt.

1644.
I love the sounds of summertime,
That take me always back in time,
To lazy days of locust song
And laundry popping on the line.

Back when I had a frame of mind
That now I very seldom find,
For dreamily I'd drift along
Those carefree days of feeling fine.

1645.
This whole idea of karma,
I wonder if it's so,
Or could a heaven or a hell
Be where, at death, we go?

Some delve the depths of dharma,
Some, seeking answers, pray,
But what's to come, we cannot tell
Till we've been whisked away.

1646.
Are the heavens cold and dead,
Or do they teem with life instead;
Does Earth stand all alone from all the rest?

If not, will we still have the gall
To sit upon our pedestal
Of thinking we, by being here, are best.

For from dead matter life began
And branched, with one branch being Man,
And we've excelled in doing what we do,

But circling some distant sun
It's likely other life's begun,
And likely life is looking out at you.

1647.
Oh you gentle summer breeze,
Come play upon my skin,
And sing a song up in the trees
While I drift out and in,

And dream a dream of long ago

When I was young and free,
For I desire, again, to know
A life lived lazily.

1648.
This world, it overwhelms us,
And inundates us all
With too much for our minds to comprehend,

While from deep down within us,
There comes a quiet call
To turn from that on which those things depend.

For that which draws attention
Is temporal at best,
And yet we hold them closest to the heart,

But they're the mind's invention;
Just matter manifest
In forms on which great meaning we impart.

1649.
Don't lock yourself in
To one way of believing;
There's much you will miss if you do,

For the box you're within
Will enlighten, while leaving
You blind to so much that is true.

1650.
The rain is falling at my feet,
I watch it and I read,
And somewhere in between the two

I find the truth I need,

For here upon this sheltered seat,
As rain and words align,
I come to understand what's true
In how the two combine.

1651.
So callous and cold and uncaring,
So cunning, controlling and cruel,
Those self-centered rulers, unsparing
Of others, who ruthlessly rule.

But worse are their fan fools who follow;
Who hold them in such high regard;
Who just cannot help but to wallow,
And worship and witlessly ward.

1652.
Few see the good in having less,
In filling up with emptiness;
In sitting still in silent solitude,

For we've been taught it's wasting time
To seek, within, the soul sublime;
That prayer is a pathetic platitude.

1653.
The setting sun is shining on my face,
The smell of fresh cut grass is in the air,
With work all done I make this quiet place,
A place to sit and rest without a care.

How good it feels when all my work is done,

And time provides an opening for me
To contemplate the slowly setting sun,
And sink into a soft serenity.

1654.
Sometimes the Muse is quiet
And leaves my head alone,
Sometimes I just cannot keep up
With all that it has shown,

But always it is present,
And always by my side,
To teach me of it's talent
And be my constant guide.

1655.
I am a wild and wailing wind,
I am a gentle breeze,
I am an ever-changing blend
Of all that's framed by these,

But now and then, upon my soul,
A stillness does descend,
To heal me from the steady toll
That's taken by the wind.

1656.
I watch them build and billow
And bloom into the sky,
Then water well this land, so dry and brown.

So dusty, and so fallow;
So deep in drought and dry,
It deeply drinks of what comes pouring down.

1657.
I sit here drifting in and out
As rain comes pouring down,
And thunder rumbles in the distant hills,

And watch this tree dance all about,
Dressed in a silver gown,
While at its roots the water runs in rills.

1658.
Make this day a day of letting go.
Release your grip and fall into the flow.
Abandon everything you think you know,
And see the world with eager, open eyes.

For you can choose to fit into the mold,
And wear it willingly until you're old,
But in your hand, that little key you hold
Will open more than you might realize.

1659.
There is a loneliness to life
Community can cure,
But often we get lost in our belonging,

For if you do not know yourself
The self will not endure,
But mold itself into the life it's longing.

1660.
Be open to believing
In ways you never knew,
And you will find epiphany
Come pouring over you,

And with it a relieving
Of that which gnawed within;
That hungering to simply be
At one with all again.

1661.
Always there'll be things to do
That will consume you through and through
If you don't turn away and turn to living,

For you've one life and this is it;
One fleeting chance to live a bit,
So turn and take the treasures life is giving.

1662.
We live in three dimensions
And that is all we know,
But science says there may be many more.

Might they be but inventions,
These truths they're seeking so,
Or could it be that crazy at the core.

1663.
Is your show of faith pretend?
Do you sometimes believe,
That on the day you meet your end,
Your life will up and leave?

That life will simply be no more
And you will cease to be?
That death's an end and not a door
Into eternity?

If so your faith is not in fault,
For faith will question all,
But if one day your doubt should halt,
Know you've built up a wall.

A wall behind which comforts call
For you to turn away,
From looking deeply into all
The doubts that come your way.

1664.
As I sink into this state
Of soft serenity,
I feel anxiety abate
And peace come over me,

And what was it that triggered this
Enlightened state of mind?
'Twas following each bit of bliss
To see what I might find.

1665.
Maybe I'm the only one
Who sees the world this way,
Maybe I'm enlightened, maybe not,

For maybe all I've done is spun
Words in a webbed array,
Within which little meaning has been caught.

1666.
If all from one point did arise
Are all bits still connected;
Entangled with each other in some way?

If so, I think we might surmise,
'Though it be not detected,
That we engage with all things when we pray.

1667.
As years pass you by, grow ancient, not old;
Grow rich in the wisdom of time,
And let, like a flower, your last days unfold
As they pass in a series sublime.

And know, 'though your body may falter and fail,
And your mind may grow simple and slow,
That the spirit within will stay healthy and hale
If your life has allowed it to grow.

1668.
If one day you tire of life
And see there nothing new,
And wear down from the constant strife
That living lays on you,

Don't turn away in deep despair,
As though your life were through,
But find new joy in what you share
And in the good you do.

1669.
Today I started thinking
Of all that could have been,
And all that I have wasted on the way,

Till in my soul a sinking
Of sadness settled in,
To dim me down with deep and dark dismay.

But how can I know something
I wish I could have done
Would have resulted as I think it would?

For maybe there is nothing
That I could have begun
That would have, in the end, turned out this good.

1670.
I see you a-standing across the way,
Your two roving eyes romancing,
What if you were to turn those eyes onto me,
Would they soon see my soul here a-dancing?

And if I were to smile, would you turn them away,
Would you leave my heart here a-beating?
Would you smile in return and walk up to me?
Would the two of us soon be a-meeting?

What if you were to place your hand into mine,
Would we two soon commence to dancing?
Would we two feel the happiness in our embrace?
Would we soon find ourselves romancing?

And what if, in our love, our two lives should combine,
To make us a life worth the living?
Now that is a path to a beautiful place;
To a long life of sweet selfless giving.

I see you a-standing across the way,
Your starry eyes all a-glowing,
For I see you've sought out and you've found your true love,
And that it isn't me I'm a-knowing.

So I'll leave you a-standing across the way,
But for your happiness I'll be praying,

For you've flown away like a beautiful dove,
That I hoped for a while would be staying.

1671.
Oh there's not a place where I want to go
If you cannot be there beside me,
For it's not the same, no it's not, don't you know,
If you're not right there walking with me.

Now once I wandered and walked all alone,
And wrapped this whole world up around me,
But then I found you and my heart made of stone
Just melted away from within me.

And now my whole heart you hold in your hand,
For I gave it freely to you,
And here by your side I will always stand,
Till my dying day takes me from you.

So take these words as a gift that I give,
As a promise I'm making to you,
To be by your side for as long as I live,
And that I'll pass away glad I knew you.

1672.
It's such a long, long way away,
And getting further every day,
While fading out into the fog of time,

Yet seems like only yesterday
That I was just a child at play;
That now is but a melancholy rhyme.

1673.
I'll take you tonight to our favorite place,
To where we are known and we're knowing
Most everyone there, at least by their face;
Where more often than not we are going.

We'll have a good meal and a drink or two,
Or more if we're feeling like drinking,
And I'll give, though the night, my attention to you,
For that's all I can give I'm a-thinking.

And though there is nothing about what we'll do,
That others might see as amazing,
Arising from all the small things we pursue
Will be this rich life we are raising.

Each day's a collection of trivial things,
With rarely a magical moment,
But it's how we put them together that brings
This bounty of beauty's bestowment.

1674.
Unannounced, just now and then,
A sinking sadness settles in;
A melancholy motion
That my heart cannot contain,

But I know I must let it flow,
For as they come, they too will go,
Like waves upon the ocean;
Like sheets of heavy rain.

1675.
Oh thank you, thank you thank you sky,
For pouring down on me,

And cooling off this awful summer day,

That was before so hot and dry,
With such humidity,
That breathing simply took my breath away.

1676.
I sit in the shade on a hot summer day,
A gentle breeze hissing around me,
While now and then nudging the wind chimes to play
A slow soothing summer song softly,

To conjure a dream of a summer gone by,
When you and I first came to knowing
Each other, and saw love in each other's eye,
Not knowing where we would be going,

And think how we found such great happiness in
The act of just being together,
And how I would certainly do it again,
For we have found joy in each other.

1677.
I love the light at break of day
That grows so gradually,
And gently probes the corners of the night,

To call the shadows out and play
Upon the canopy,
And bathe the upper leaves in loving light.

1678.
Is magic something that is real?
My heart says maybe so,

Though not the magic you believe to be.

For I believe and fully feel
That some things do not show,
But touch at times on our reality.

1679.
You are the fount from which does flow
The force that frames this world you know,
And fills that frame with joy or misery,

For though things happen as they may,
And fate can flow whichever way,
You always have a hand in what will be.

1680.
The world will get along just fine
Without you being in it,
It may, in fact, do better with you gone.

If that is so seek out a sign
That has direction to it;
That gives a goal to set your sights upon.

1681.
Summer to me was a cool, running stream
With water so clear I could see,
Each minnow and pebble that lay far below
As though they were all right under me,

And each lazy day of the summer would seem
To be better than all of the rest,
And pass by so sweetly and simple and slow,
That each seemed it must be the best.

1682.
Oh how the echo of that hateful ideology
Still lingers as a loss across the land.
But though it left a wicked wound upon society,
We've showed resolve by healing hand-in-hand.

1683.
Out on the porch the rain fell all around me,
While thunder rolled and rumbled all around,
And listening, I fell to sleeping soundly
While soothed and serenaded by the sound.

And there I dreamt a drifting dream remembered
But vaguely when out of it I awoke
Abruptly by a bolt that flashed and thundered,
That blew the dream away like drifting smoke.

1684.
Do you feel your destiny
Has limits placed upon it
By those who see the color of your skin

As ranking in society,
And how you fit within it,
And that you lost before you could begin?

It's true, you know, and terrible,
And somehow we must fix it,
But nothing can put right the poisoned past,

Just know, though, you're unbreakable
And you can stand up to it
By shattering the mold in which you're cast.

1685.
Your life, it forms a fabric
With patterns that portray
A panoramic portraiture of you,

Whose panes depict your rubric;
Your purpose and the way
You've lived your life to make it all come true.

1686.
Knitted by hand, and made with love,
And graced with goodness from above,
The fabric of your life's a precious thing,

For it's the cloth from which is sewn
The self you wear and call your own,
Through which is filtered always everything.

But is your fabric made by hand,
Or is it artificial, canned,
And copied from the social sites you see?

If you discover that is how
It is, take up your needle now
And sew some individuality.

1687.
I have no anger in me,
No rant I must release,
Just sadness every time I see
A punctuated peace,

That's halted by the hand of hate
That comes continually,
Out of the sad and sorry state

Of our society.

1688.
I want to be a friend to you,
To know you fully, through and through;
To feel your feelings deeply in my heart.

For life's too long to live alone
And every day spent on your own,
You're missing out on life's most precious part.

1689.
When catastrophe occurs
Where will your focus be,
On making sure your stash endures
Or sharing selflessly?

And what, with nothing left to you
But hunger and despair,
Would you hope those with more would do,
To hoard and hide, or share?

1690.
You have in you the power to
Create a paradise,
Both for yourself and others that you meet,

And all that you have got to do
Is simply treat them nice;
Is give the gift of goodness when you greet.

1691.
Sometimes life is sudden,

And slaps you in the face,
Sometimes life, lived leisurely,
Preserves a pleasant pace,

But always life is bidden
To change from day to day,
And let the law of entropy
Point out the one true way.

1692.
What is it that defines you?
Is it a thing that's real?
Do artificial attributes
Affix to how you feel

The terms you're tightly tied to,
That label who you are?
If so, cling tightly to your roots
And cast what's fake afar.

1693.
Just as the timbers of a cross
Meet at one point of balance,
Our lives and pure perfection intersect,

And when they do all pain and loss
Are eased up by the essence
Of goodness that such balanced lives project.

1694.
These gentle rills have formed these hills
One pebble at a time,
And given them their personality.

As we have grown into our own
Out of the simple slime,
Through changes far too slow for us to see.

1695.
I walk through these woods on a late summer day
And think of who walked here before me,
Who lived here before they were driven away
By white man for greed and for glory,

Who came from the hunt to see smoke in the air,
And find, at home, all dead or dying,
And I think, what a shame that we're not taught to care;
That it's masked by omission or lying.

1696.
It seems like everyone these days
Is walking 'round us in a haze,
And are, to what lies right before them, blind.

For when they stare at their display
For treasures lost, they lose their way,
Tricked by the trail of trinkets that they find.

1697.
The morning tells me all I need to know,
For to its pace I set my life to flow,
A pace that I maintain throughout the day,
That centers me when life gets in the way.

1698.
When there's little left of me
I hope I'm like the moon;

That waning silver sliver of delight,

That peeks out from behind a tree
And, slowly setting, croon
Till stars come out and join it in the night.

1699.
It's those you touch with love in life,
Who do the same in turn,
That end up being your true legacy,

For everyone you know is rife
With aptitude to learn,
From your example, to live lovingly.

1700.
I truly love a rainy day,
It makes me introspective,
Which works to wash my worries all away,

And what I find, deep down inside,
When being more reflective,
Are all the simple truths I must abide.

1701.
The way we label instantly
The people that we meet,
The way we posture purposely
Before we go to greet,

The way that we interpret things
To fit with our charade,
Distorts the truth and always brings
Malaise from what we've made.

1702.
Each moment's an eternity;
Eternity's the time
It takes as each brief passing point elapses.

And all I think and do and see
Lives in the bubble I'm
Now in, until the next, when it collapses.

1703.
The things you want are vain and evanescent;
Just think of what you yearned for in the past,
That matter not a bit here in the present.
So why think what you long for now will last?

It's hard, you know, to sit in perfect silence,
And not be drawn away by your desire,
But only emptiness achieves the balance
That when attained becomes your true attire.

1704.
Pale blue and pink,
The sky does sink
Into the black of night,

And as it does
I watch because
It's such a splendid sight.

Rose red and black
When it comes back
To greet me in the morn,

When once again
The world does spin

And we are both reborn.

1705.
You are who you know you are,
Though they say otherwise,
For you're a brilliant, shining star,
So take off that disguise,

That you have worn to keep them all
From seeing what is real,
And stand before them, proud and tall,
And show them how you feel.

1706.
The goodness people see in you
Will grow out of the works you do,
Not from the platitudes that you profess,

For it's the heart that moves the hands
To do, with love, what love commands,
That matters, not the people you impress.

1707.
Only by the loss of self
Can what you seek be found;
Yes, only emptiness will show the way,

So put your ego on a shelf
And be no longer bound
To what you were, and find yourself today.

1708.
Your task in life is finding

Which tasks you should pursue,
To make sense of what seems to be a mess,

For there's one thread that's winding
Through life whose trail is true,
While all the rest are simply meaningless.

1709.
Live here and now with a heart full of love,
Though it's easy to live in the past,
Or hope for a future that you're dreaming of,
For the moment you're in will not last

Beyond the brief instant that you are now in,
This moment of crisp clarity,
So live it in full ere the next one begin
And it's put away permanently.

1710.
Tell me now, what matters,
What meaning can be found,
If in the end we all must pass away?

I've torn this thing to tatters,
While searching for what's sound,
And found a tiny whisper of a way

To give my life a meaning,
And sanctify my soul,
That says to focus living to align

With other lives convening
Towards a common goal
Of realizing love in life's design.

1711.
Our earth cries out a silent scream
That we choose to ignore,
And likely will until it's far too late,

For verdant fields might be a dream
Where we will walk no more,
If we don't make this ignorance abate.

1712.
You think our time is running out,
But we've eternity;
I know it when I look into your eyes,

And see that life is all about
The perpetuity
Of magic moments we eternalize.

1713.
Kindness is a cancer,
But ever so benign,
For though it spreads without control
It's side effects are fine,

But hatred is an ember,
So soon to be a blaze
Unless extinguished by the soul,
For only love allays.

1714.
Tethered to eternity,
We see the self unceasing,
And borne within the body but a bit,

But what if this reality,
Of birth and long releasing,
Is all that there will ever be of it.

If so, from what is meaning made?
Is it just wishful wanting
We do to dampen down the dread of death?

I feel I must, before I fade,
Resolve this hopeless haunting,
So I, in peace, can take my final breath.

Faith, I've found, will take me far;
Will give me hope and healing,
And point me down the path I should pursue,

For faith assures us that we are
Not all alone in dealing
With life; that we have help in all we do.

And faith holds out a hand of hope
That there'll be something after;
That somehow we'll continue to exist,

Which helps the faithful ones to cope
And meet their end with laughter,
But scientific thought says to resist.

For science shows, convincingly,
How life could be created,
And how the sense of self could come about

From mindless matter naturally,
With points all well debated,
And that it could be so I have no doubt.

But science sees no sight or sign

Of afterlife existence,
Eliminating hope for a reprieve

From life; no final finish line
That crossed, with long persistence
On living right, rewards those who believe.

So meaning based on what will be
Beyond this life I'm living,
Is tainted by the doggedness of doubt,

That nags and nudges constantly
And shows no sign of giving
A ear to what my faith is all about.

Thus once again, where I do I find
The meaning that I must;
Where lies that one illuminating light?

Might I have all along been blind,
And only need to trust
That meaning's simply found in doing right?

1715.
Looking at free will
From a reductionist perspective
Just makes me feel so void of self inside,

And yet, it cannot kill
This thing I know, when I'm reflective;
That sense that I've a soul that can decide.

So what am I to do
With all this dissonance within me?
Am I to pick a side on which to fight,

When what I feel as true
Might seem as such from hoping only,
For truth to be the side I wish were right?

So though I'm racked with doubt
The thing I feel about my freedom
Is that I have a mind that can decide,

And how that comes about,
Be it through choice or algorithm,
The fact that I've free will feels real inside.

1716.
How is it that a sunset,
How is it that a smile,
How is it that a memory
Can last for such a while?

How can it be that we get
So much from things so small?
How wonderful the way that we
See magic in it all.

1717.
There is a light that lives within,
That animates this sack of skin,
And brings to life the matter it contains.

Of course, there is no way to prove
It's there, and yet when I remove
The rest of me that little light remains.

1718.
Just how does a baby grow up to be bad;

To harbor such hideous hate?
What turned them away from the goodness they had;
What made their bare beauty abate?

You never can know, so when I am harassed
I try to remain undefiled,
And patiently wait til their anger has passed,
And think how once they were a child.

1719.
Love ignites this lamp of mine
That then illuminates
All others with its soft and gentle glow,

Whose radiating rays define
Each face, and permeates
Into the soul of everyone I know.

To light the lamp of love within,
That each might pass along
Their love to those they meet along the way,

And help them reach that moment when
We all at last belong
Together where we hoped to be one day.

1720.
In this field of fern and flower
I detect a potent power
Pulling life up from the rocky soil.

An ancient action, never ceasing,
Of new birth and slow releasing,
Though an endless task of tireless toil.

Each bud that I behold is bearing;
Every stem and stalk is wearing
Gifts of wonder for us to behold.

So seek this thing of which I'm speaking
That, through your unceasing seeking,
You'll find youth before you get too old.

1721.
Our shared beliefs connect as one
These lives of subjectivity,
And show, through ancient stories spun
With care and creativity,

How similar we are inside,
How close our commonality,
And calls, with others to confide
In shared spirituality.

1722.
For what potential purpose was our creativity?
How did it aid our struggle to survive?
And why waste precious time on my poetic tendency?
Why give in to this unrelenting drive

To bring my life alive in these alliterative lines,
That delve into the deeper depths of me?
Is it to cast this life I live out in a light that shines
Along the length of immortality?

1723.
When you break down a living thing
As far as it will go,
You'll not discover life's sole source and cause,

For you'll find nothing there to bring
About the life you know,
Just lifeless matter bound to rigid laws.

And as you work your way back out,
Through ever growing size,
It's not until you reach the top you'll find,

The form of life you know about;
The form you realize;
The living thing with heart and soul and mind.

We're made of molecules that mesh
Together by design
To form our cells and doing so define,

These bodies we're embodied by,
To which we each align
So tightly to, and see as yours and mine.

Just lose a limb and you remain,
Though less, the one you were;
Identity, it seems withstands a lot,

But when there's damage to the brain
The self may not endure;
May change into a thing that it was not.

So it would seem the brain must be
The very source we seek;
Must be the center where the self does sit,

And that our whole reality,
The self of which we speak,
Originates and rises out of it.

Such thinking makes a lot of sense,

For science sees it so,
And I can't help but listen and concur,

But always I am on the fence
Between the facts I know,
And that which all these feelings felt infer.

For it does surely seem to me
That there is something here
Transcending that which matter could emit,

A feeling of eternity
Behind the now so near;
A knowing that my words cannot transmit.

But what it is must coexist
With scientific thought,
If I am to embrace wholeheartedly

It's precepts, and to you insist
That what it is I sought
Was found by looking deep inside of me.

1724.
To feel a thought wholeheartedly,
And sense it through and through,
Is what it means to truly be alive,

And caught, through creativity,
As art, it gives a view
Into the very depths in which you dive.
That sea of subjectivity,
So vast and deep and wide,
In which we live and where we've always been,

Is captured in the art that we

Create when we decide
To share what we experience within.

1725.
We're made of molecules that mesh
Together by design,
To form the cells that form the flesh,
And so we must define

Our bodies as assemblages,
From lifeless matter made;
Each born and briefly flourishes,
Each fated fast to fade.

But where's the life within it all?
Where burns the fire we feel?
By looking at the very small
Do we miss what is real?

There's life, of course, in every cell,
But that's not what we seek,
It is this life we know so well
Of which we've come to speak.

These lives of pure and perfect peace,
These lives of wailing woe,
These lives we wish would never cease
And mourn for when they go.

So deep and full and meaningful,
It seems they must transcend
The purview of the particle,
But nature's laws don't bend.

Just look at what those laws achieve,
How can we contradict

Such laws with things that we believe
When they so well predict?

And that is true when thinking in
Reductionistic ways,
For objectivity has been,
Through time, the path that pays.

But there's another currency
We value so much more,
That's gained through subjectivity;
There's what we're looking for,

For there are inner laws that we
Have yet to understand,
Explaining what we know to be
As glorious and grand.

And it is in the inner mind,
Where truths so softly speak,
That each, in their own way, must find
The meaning that they seek.

1726.
There is a light that shines within
And when you find it there,
You'll look back out upon the world
And see it everywhere,

For there's a little lamp of tin
That's waiting to be found,
Whose light, when it's at last unfurled
Will light all that's around.

1727.
Some see faith as nothing but
A following of fools
Whose eyes, to modern thought, are shut
And blindly follow rules

Laid down so very long ago
That they no more apply,
But those with faith know what they know
And will, if you ask why,

Explain that it seems very real,
For from their faith does flow,
Strong streams of light and love that feel
In line with what they know.

1728.
Some feel that faith is folly, for
No prayer or wishful thinking
Can change what science says will come to be,

Yet I believe that there is more;
That there exists a linking
That ties us each to true transcendency.

And what that is I cannot say,
But it's a forceful feeling
That flows from open hearts continually,

And will, until our dying day,
Wash each with hope and healing,
To carry us into eternity.

1729.
It's all so evanescent,

This moment that you're in.
This day, this year, this life you'll live,
This world on which you spin.

But here, within the present,
Where time comes to a stall,
You'll find the miracles that give
Such meaning to it all.

1730.
The closer that we get to understanding
A single thing, the less we seem to know,
And yet our minds are constantly demanding
That all that has been hidden here should show.

It is this constant yearning that defines us;
This steady search for common clarity,
But it's our frequent failures that remind us
We're not amid a minor mystery.

Our fault lies in a failing of our focus
To target on the world that lies within,
And search for all our answers at the locus
Where we are now and we have always been.

For we'll not find the answers looking outward,
Though what lies there is meaningful and real,
But by a reexamination inward
Of what lies at the root of how we feel.

1731.
You have inside a nagging need
To join with those like-minded,
For it is in your nature to belong,

But take great care, lest you should ceed
Your soul and thus be blinded,
And not see what you're following is wrong.

1732.
While fearful of the future
And pining for the past
We often miss what we are living for,

For it is in our nature
To make each moment last
By contemplating them when they're no more,

And we are built to ponder
The possibilities
And plan for that which may or may not be,

But though the mind may wander
It's crucial that it seize
The fleeting stillness of reality.

1733.
Here today and gone tomorrow,
Born to joy you'll leave to sorrow;
Between the two, what wonder will there be?

Will you fill in the time you're given
Curious and ever driven
To explore each possibility?

Will your mind be wide or narrow?
Will you aim be like an arrow,
Aimed upon one tiny point of view?

Or will it be wide and sweeping,

Always watching, never sleeping,
Redefining always what is true?

1734.
What anchors do you drag behind,
To which your boat is bound?
If you looked back would you there find
You cling to what you found,

That mattered then but does no more
Have meaning for your mind?
If so, cut loose and leave the shore
Of that lost land behind.

1735.
Things have changed dramatically;
Things are not what they were,
Yet I believe emphatically
That goodness will endure,

For through the whole of history,
As evil ebbed and flowed,
The good have tended carefully
The seeds of love they sowed.

1736.
We all long for longevity
And hope for an acuity
Of mind until at last we pass away.

We hope for health until we die,
And when it fails we wonder why
We couldn't have just one more healthy day.

For we assume that we will be
Forever hale, and healthily
Inhabit, till we die, ourselves as such.

But fitness falters by-and-by,
Since all who live are bound to die;
Just hope that death will have a gentle touch.

1737.
I am, I do believe, the only one
Who feels the burning of the setting sun,
The way I feel it burning on my face,

And that no other knows the world as I,
For each sees slightly different through their eye,
And each lives in a slightly different place.

For I believe a part of what we feel
Within ourselves to be so very real,
Is simply fabricated by the mind,

And that the knowing that we all beseech,
Will be, while we're embodied, out of reach,
Such that we'll always be a little blind.

Though there's a common world in which we live
Which we perceive through what the senses give,
That world is filtered through in different ways,

And what we sense as our reality
Is not sensed by all others equally,
For each perceives a slightly different phase.

And it is in that shifting of what's real,
That gives each life it's own distinctive feel
That falsely we assume all others share,

For in the end you're not the same as I,
And will not be until the day we die,
When we, released, are beautiful and bare.

1738.
It rained two days, but when I woke
The morning sun was shining,
So I pulled on my boots and took to trail,

To once again cast off the yoke
Put on by my defining
These worldly things to be the holy grail.

The leaves above were damp with dew
That dripped as I went walking
Below a canopy of green and gold,

And I perceived that what is true
Cannot be told by talking,
But must, in silent solitude, unfold.

1739.
The moon is full and falling fast
Behind the western trees,
The eastern sky is hinting of the dawn,

And knowing that it will not last
I turn back west to seize
The moon go down, but it's already gone.

So quickly does each moment pass,
That if you blink an eye
You'll likely miss the ones that matter most,

And all the others you amass,

As meaning passes by,
Will seem for naught when you give up the ghost.

So take each moment moving by
And live it like your last,
To find in each the gifts it has to give,

For every one will quickly fly
From present to the past,
And in each you've but one brief chance to live.

1740.
Upon the bush that bloomed so bright
Just one red rose remains,
Reminding me of days forever gone,

And as I slip into the night
I hope my mind retains
Its memory to help me carry on.

For winter's surely on its way,
With darkness drawing near,
Defining life as dimmer days descend,

But as the daylight slips away
I'll hold that vision dear
To give me hope that winter's way will end.

1741.
May one day your eyes be open and bright
To see through the veil of self serving,
May one day you choose to set your life right
And straighten the path that's been curving.

May you hear the calling before it's too late,

And change the direction you're heading,
For you must, if you are to set your life straight,
Abandon the trail you are treading.

1742.
When you learn to live with less
You'll find there's so much more,
For as you fill the emptiness
You cover up the core

Where all the things that matter lay,
Just waiting to be found,
But with your wantings washed away
You'll be no longer bound

To ends that justify the means,
But do not mean a thing,
So wake and walk the way that weans
You off your hungering.

1743.
Life is like a morning sky;
It cannot be contained,
Its beauty grows and changes constantly,

But of that beauty, if you try
To deem it as ordained,
You'll feel lost when life lingers listlessly.

So revel in the morning bloom,
But on the darker days
Know that the sun still shines behind it all,

To filter through the morning gloom
And touch, with light, the haze,

For beauty can be delicate and small.

1744.
Each life is a brief blossoming
Of brain and bone and skin,
From which comes the reality
That rises from within,

As mix of objectivity,
Defining all we see,
And unexplained epiphany
That touches tenderly.

And where the two combine as one,
With depth and dissonance,
Is where the song of soul is spun;
Is where we go to dance.

1745.
Live in the moment and see where it goes;
You might be surprised in the end,
Not by the last leg of the path that you chose,
But by what lay around every bend.

For the living you do in the life that you lead
Is a lingering lyrical lay,
Whose words tell the story of how you proceed
And the wonders you found on the way.

It's a song that you've sung since your journey began
That has been, all along, improvised,
And continues to follow no predefined plan
But to be of the moment comprised.

1746.
The life that you live is a long, lovely lay,
That sings of the sky at the break of the day,
And tells of the wonders you found on the way
To where your long life has been leading.

And though every new line derives from the last,
And is in the shape of the former one cast,
The influence wanes as lines move to the past,
Their memory slowly receding.

And all that you are is the sound of that song,
Combined as the voices you sang all along,
And though some, at times, might have hit a note wrong
Or sang out in a troubling tone,

The song you sing now, if you sing from the heart,
Can call out what's wrong and proclaim a new start,
For what you sing now's the most pertinent part;
If what you sing now is your own.

1747.
How little can you live with, yet
Live your life happily?
How close to nothing can you get
Before you cease to be?

Will you find in your emptiness
What means could not provide,
And have with nothing, nothing less
Than your life satisfied?

1748.
These words, they must stand on their own,
There's nothing more here to be shown;

These words are all I have for you to see,

So read them as they are and find
What they become within your mind,
When they resound in your reality.

1749.
Focus yourself on one moment of mind;
On one thought or one feeling you feel.
Forget all the rest for a bit just to find
Why it seems such a point of appeal.

Does it still shine as bright, there apart from the rest;
Does it seem it can stand on its own?
For it's only pure love that can tackle that test,
So seek that till its shining is shown.

1750.
The Muse makes a magical moment
From the moments we mark as mundane,
By giving a voice to the present
That follows us as its refrain.

It forms in us first as a feeling,
Then gathers up words as it goes,
Describing the depths our dealing
With life, from which poetry flows.

1751.
We all attempt to understand
The world in our own way,
And do our best to make it on our own,

By walking lone along the strand

Just at the break of day,
Until the light of wakefulness has grown,

Where we can see the others there,
Bare feet below the foam,
Who too are drawn to meet the rising sun,

Who give us what they have to share
From where their feet did roam,
From which our common paradigm is spun,

And that is good, to join and share
And build a common bond
Of understanding that we all have known,

But don't forget the beauty bare
The dimmest dawn has donned,
When all alone you've watched as grandeur's grown.

1752.
I stepped outside the house today
To see the sun arising
And watch the morning colors play
Upon the far horizon.

While sunbeams touch the tops of trees,
With cooling coffee steaming,
I felt the dawn brew up a breeze
To wake me from my dreaming.

1753.
Long ago, when I was young
I sang a song that's not been sung
For years, and maybe will not be again,

For I'm not who I used to be,
I changed that voluntarily
To leave behind the person I had been,

But who I was is with me still,
And wanders there upon the hill
Of history, that I have left behind,

And I can hear it now and then,
That song, I sang, from way back when
Still echo in the foothills of my mind.

1754.
Some days are drab and dreary,
While some dawn decked with dew.
On some you wake still weary;
On others, fresh and new.

One day your days here started
And one day they will cease,
And you'll be ever parted
From it all with that release.

So live the ones worth living
And bear those that are bad,
And share with selfless giving
Of the joys that you have had.

1755.
What is the ultimate source of your soul;
Does it come from without or within?
Does it come only once, to make the flesh whole,
Or revisit again and again?

Or is it your being is born of the brain,

Out of which your whole self does arise?
It's one or the other, or both; it's not plain
From the words that you've read from the wise.

But what do you find when you let the words go,
And you've found what it feels to be you?
What is there when you set aside all that you know
In pursuit of one thing that is true?

Do you find there a knowing you cannot express;
A point you can circle around,
That when put into words is no more than a guess,
But becomes for you all when it's found?

1756.
Your troubles can seem bigger, like
The moon on the horizon,
That later in the night seems far away.

Just know concerns will always spike
As worries are arising,
Then fade as other comforts come your way.

1757.
When the wind is blowing cold
And trees are bleak and bare,
Think of the waiting sprouts that hold
Springs promise, green and fair;

Of how they lay beneath the ground
Awaiting to arise,
When waning winter's warmth is found,
To bloom before your eyes.

1758.
I love the way the rising sun
Casts light into the trees,
To touch the top of every one,
Then spread down to their knees,

I love the way it lingers long,
Until the sky is bright,
To mingle with the dying song
Of fast receding night

1759.
Embrace the hungers when they come,
But don't let them control you;
Take from them what you need to carry on,

For in the end you are the sum
Of all the things that you do,
So take what's good and let the rest be gone.

1760.
Whispers in the treetops,
Sparkles in the dew,
Ripples in the quiet stream
Combine inside of you

Each day like diamond dewdrops,
With all the world within,
Reflecting outwardly the dream
Of all you've ever been.

1761.
Morning means so much to me,
With endless possibility,

I feel reborn each time I see
The ruddy red of dawn,

And in the newly minted day
I find the long-forgotten way;
The path to peace, for which I pray,
To set myself upon.

1762.
Your dreams are really all you've got;
They bring the living light,
For without dreams your world is not
A wonder, fresh and bright,

But is an endless drudgery
Of trying to survive,
So dream a rich reality,
And in it come alive.

1763.
To keep your soul salubrious,
Make sure to water well
The verdant vines and meadows of your mind,

And sing songs slow and sonorous,
That echo down the dell
To tell the tale of what you've come to find.

1764.
My mind is as smooth as a cold winter lake
As I near the first day of December,
No ripple or rill does my consciousness make,
But, reflecting from it, I remember,

A magical moment from long, long ago,
Floating up from the depths of remembrance,
Then sink to the bottom and no longer show,
On the surface, a sign or a semblance.

1765.
I have you here, right in my heart,
Where you will always be,
For death will not break us apart;
We're bound eternally.

We're bound by love, which makes us one
In spirit, such that we
Will carry on what we've begun
For all eternity.

1766.
A cotton candy sunrise,
A thin, forgotten moon,
A moment that will never come again.

Such beauties fall on our eyes,
But pass away too soon,
So live for now, not what's to be or been.

1767.
Awake and arise,
For your time here is passing;
Your moments are slipping away,

So to see and surmise,
What you have been amassing
And throw what means nothing away.

1768.
I woke and watched the world awake,
It breathed a breeze, the leaves to shake;
It spread a light that crept into the dell.

And from the breeze, the sound, the light,
It gave to me these words I write
To capture and convey its sacred spell.

1769.
I sing a song of seasons,
A song of earth and sky,
That flows from me like water from a well.

Don't ask me for my reasons,
I could not tell you why,
I only know I cannot shake the spell.

For spell it is I'm under,
And one I can't contain,
So awed am I at all that I perceive,

For all the world's a wonder,
From grand to most mundane,
And I must wend my words throughout its weave.

1770.
No matter how you fudge the facts,
The world as it is now
Was built upon self-centered genocide,

And carried out through countless acts
With no regard to how
Such acts impacted on the other side.

With power pulled into one point
It's join or waste away,
And that is how they justified their deeds,

And why they felt they must anoint,
And follow every day,
Their leaders to fulfill their nagging needs.

Do you think you could turn away
From what you follow now,
If you saw the destruction in your wake?

Or would you look the other way
Lest you awake to how
You must turn from the path you chose to take?

1771.
When all my leaves have fallen
And I am old and gray,
Don't think that there is nothing left inside,

For though my soul seems sullen,
Know deep within I pray
That you would simply sit here at my side.

1772.
Through comfort and complacency
We think the world is well,
And feel we're not responsible
For someone else's Hell,

For we've an ideology
Of ruling all the rest,
With deeds deemed justifiable,
Since we know what is best:

The freedoms of democracy,
Where one can build a nation
Upon the tenets we've been taught
Of self-determination,

And individuality;
Both noble goals indeed,
But truth be told, we've often fought
To meet some corporate need.

We've seized the land and livelihood
Of those caught in the way
All for, we're told, the betterment
They'll realize one day.

And from their loss our lives are good,
Though it's come at a cost
That we perceive as blood well spent,
And hold the lives we've lost

As heroes who have given all,
As they have surely done,
Which led, through their self-sacrifice
To battles sorely won,

But they're the pawns who heard the call
And followed faithfully;
Just tools to carry out the vice
Of corporate policy.

For we are not a nation free,
We're just a people proud,
Who cannot see what we enjoy
Was taken, not endowed;

Who, in the name of liberty,
Have shipped to foreign shores,

Where we've released and still employ
A endless wave of wars,

Waged in the name of greater good,
While taking what they had,
And claiming all the while that they
Should for it all be glad.

But though the fact's well understood
That there's a debt we owe,
We claim it's one we cannot pay
And they should let it go;

We claim those crimes had all been cast
Before we came along,
And though to take their land away
Most certainly was wrong,

That we can't change the poisoned past
Or mend the wrongs we've done,
But that rings true no more today
Those are but lies we've spun,

To kindly cover up and cast
Our actions in a light,
That sweeps the weight of guilt away
And makes them all seem right.

1773.
Do you recall the way life was
Before you lost the magic;
Before you had it all so figured out?

It ought to make you sad because
A childhood's end is tragic,
When wonder is replaced by dogged doubt.

1774.
Your life's enlivened by your dreams,
They are the means that move you,
So let them lead you, for it seems,
To follow would behoove you.

Just follow them to where they lead,
And trust in what they show you,
For they will give you all you need
That you might come to know you.

1775.
The world you know is who you are,
The two are tightly bound;
There is no crisp and clear dividing line.

For you're a rare and shining star
And also you're the ground;
You are what happens when the two entwine.

And yet to tear the two apart
Is what we tend to do,
As we seek out the essence of the soul,

But you will find that when you start
To separate the two,
By doing so you are no longer whole.

For every part depends upon
The presence of the rest,
And none can stay alive for long alone,

For you have been, right from the dawn
Of life, both bathed and blessed
With spirit tightly bound to flesh and bone.

1776.
You're touched at times by memory,
Like rain upon the skin,
That wakes a rich reality
That you can live again.

For though you live the here and now
The past is always near
And often comes alive somehow
To draw a smile or tear.

1777.
My life is a wade through a river of words
That flow from the mountains of mind,
Where thoughts and ideas from the authors I've heard
Stream down and are quickly combined,

To run like a terrible torrent at times,
Or move with the gentlest flow,
And from it I draw the cool waters of rhyme
That tell of these currents I know.

1778.
You leave a deep impression,
With everything you do;
Your print remains on everything you touch,

For every intercession
Affects much more than you,
So keep in mind your actions matter much.

1779.
Seek in the world the chord that plays
The music of your soul,

For therein you will know true peace of mind,

Lest you spend all your precious days
In chasing down a goal
That doesn't play the song you hope to find.

1780.
There is a chord that's yours alone
That no one else can play;
A tune to which your spirit sweetly sings.

So play it loud, that you be known,
To others by the way
The song of self you sing so rightly rings.

1781.
I sought a nascent knowing
That transcended understanding,
As faith to tie me to eternity,

And found it ever flowing
When I gave up on demanding
That I perceive it all with clarity,

For diving into dogma
Gave me hints of the direction
That I should take to find the sign I sought,

But in the end the aura
Of pure peace shone with perfection,
When I had turned from all that I'd been taught.

1782.
A cold, cold rain is falling down,

The sky is dull and gray,
And though the world is bare and brown
I'm filled with joy today.

I'm filled with joy for I can see
The beauty, brown and bare,
That waits forever, patiently,
To blossom everywhere.

1783.
This mid-December madness,
That leads to stress and sadness;
It seems to me an artificial thing,

That taints this time of waiting
And brings an unabating,
Cacophony into the song we sing.

1784.
What good are piety and prayer
When focused on salvation?
Just posturing and sad soliloquy.

For if you pray but do not care
For creatures of creation,
Your actions verge on vacant vanity.

1785.
Here you are; what happened
Has happened in the past.
Will you allow the echoes
Of what laid you low to last?

For every time you listen

You amplify the sound,
Which makes it echo louder
Till you hear it all around.

But if you turn attention
In full towards today,
You'll find the echoes, when ignored,
Will dim and fade away.

1786.
Behind those vacant eyes there lies
An infinite abyss,
Where cold winds wail and darkness swallows all,

Where sad souls suffer silently,
Amid the emptiness,
With woe, for they, without the wherewithal

To overcome the lack of light
Have given up all hope,
And wander lost and lonely in the dark,

But you, who have so much to share,
Can help them all to cope
By giving of your light a little spark,

For just a spark is all it takes
To drive the dark away,
And set the briars and brambles all afire,

So light their world with kindliness
To bring a brighter day,
For you've the light to send their spirits higher.

1787.
It's not the gifts beneath the tree,
It's not the decorations,
It's not the thoughtful presents we receive.

It's how for one brief moment we
Move past the preparations,
And come, each in our own way, to believe.

1788.
We're made up of the many moods that make us
The ever-changing creatures that we are,
The waves of woe that bottle up to break us,
The jewels of joy, each shining like a star.

But anchoring it all there is the constant
And never-changing self-identity,
Around which moods are moving every instant,
So center there and set your feelings free.

1789.
This misty morning magic makes
The sunrise seem surreal,
And softens, as the world awakes,
The light, to make it feel

As though it flowed out of the earth,
Arising from the root,
To give the day a gentle birth
Then shine from every shoot.

1790.
You were never satisfied,
You could not be contained,

Your life was always driven by your dreams,

But since your passing I have tried
To seek what you refrained
From pausing for while reaching the extremes.

1791.
Oh tell me brother, won't you,
What led to your demise?
What took your life, with you so strong and hale?

For right away they burned you,
Before we could surmise,
Whatever might have made your flesh to fail.

And with no chance to see you
Once you had passed away,
I feel I never got to say goodbye,

So I have not released you,
And feel you here today
As if I only dreamed you came to die.

1792.
Your life's a thread that's wove into
A tight knit tapestry,
And you're the hand that pulls the needle through,

And you decide, by what you do,
The pattern that we see,
And what it is that pattern says of you.

1793.
You're not the voice inside your head

That tells you what to do,
You're not the flesh that acts those actions out,

You're what is left when those are dead;
That's all there is of you,
And learning that is what your life's about.

1794.
We each have, deep within us,
The lives that we have known;
The pleasures and the tall plateaus of pain,

And they can overwhelm us
When we are all alone,
As we relive the moments they contain,

But they are simply shadows
Of things that will not fade;
Just empty echoes pointing to the past,

Like waves that sweep the shallows
Through which we slowly wade,
To flow across our feet till each has passed.

1795.
Be a watcher of the world
And not a servant to it;
Do not allow events to drag you in,

For what will be, will be unfurled
Without your latching to it;
Just sit in silent peace amid the din.

1796.
You are the one who watches,
The one who is aware,
You're not the thoughts or feelings
Or the things you see out there.

You are the soul that searches
And seeks serenity;
Who, in the din of dealings
With the world, hears harmony.

1797.
What is it you are looking for;
What do you hope to find?
Do you believe there might be more
Than that which moves your mind?

That you have only just begun
To touch upon the truth,
And hope, before your days are done;
Before you're long of tooth,

To see a sign of certainty
That indicates the way,
And take it towards eternity
From that decisive day?

1798.
Just let them pass unhindered,
Those things that make you grieve;
Just open up your heart and let them through,

Lest, closed, your heart be rendered
Unable to receive
The unrelenting love that comes to you.

1799.
This world that you know, and all that is in it,
Is but a brief bubble of being,
Whose surface reflects a distorted facade of what's real,

And yet you assume, when you look upon it,
That all of the things you are seeing,
And all that arises out of it as feelings you feel,

Is all that there is, for it's how you see it
As you get drawn into that dream,
And you lose all sense of the self as a separate soul,

But if you let go and stay centered outside it,
Your thoughts and your feelings will seem,
Like things to observe while the self remains healthy and whole.

1800.
Just beyond this world you see
There lies a vast infinity,
That waits for the enlightened to explore.

And how attain that heightened state;
That wonderment for which you wait?
Just face your fears and open every door.

1801.
This I know with certainty:
That nothing can be known,
Except that when we die that we
Will leave at last alone,

For we'll release the hand we hold
And let the voices go,
As we float off into the fold

To come at last to know.

1802.
It's these two things I know to be:
That death will come one day for me,
And nothing's known with certainty
Except for that one thing.

1803.
Above all else seek happiness,
For joy from that will spring,
Though life delivers constant stress,
And waves of suffering,

Those do not rise up out of life,
But from the way that we
Create from life that steady strife
By clinging desperately,

Or by resisting, either way
Your actions generate,
Duress when life does not obey
Your feats to fix your fate.

But if, when joy cannot be found,
You look instead at why
You've set demands to which it's bound,
You'll see it passes by

Because you do not let life flow,
And maybe come to see,
That if you simply let things go
You'd live life happily.

1804.
You are not the thoughts you think,
And not the moods you're feeling,
You're simply that which of those are aware,

So when you sense your spirit sink,
And feel what's real is reeling,
Remember that you're not what lies out there.

1805.
I look up through the branches bare
At bright, unbroken blue,
On this crisp, cold and cloudless winter day,

And see the patterns painted there
While I, without a clue,
Read meaning into how they shift and sway.

This tendency to tokenize;
To label and explain,
Comes from my need to own this world I see,

And thus I overanalyze,
With models in my brain
Of what are simply branches in a tree.

1806.
Happiness rains down on you,
But joy wells from within,
When you become receptive to
The beauty that has been

Forever at the root of all,
So hearken with your heart,
That you might hear its quiet call

And open to its art.

1807.
Joy is the natural state of the soul,
But it's dampened by dogged desire,
Which makes us believe we are no longer whole,
As it raises all our goals ever higher.

But when we release what we yearn to attain;
When we let what we're groping for go,
We find endless joy in the things that remain
And experience happiness grow.

1808.
You'll now and then fall deep into
The darkness of despair,
Which swallows up the lovely light of living,

But if you keep in mind that you
Can shine your love down there,
You'll find your way back from the light it's giving.

1809.
Live in this world, but don't let it change you
From who you are deep down inside,
By pulling you in and turning you into
A pile-up of passion and pride.

All that you see is finite and fleeting,
But you are an infinite sky,
So when you're immersed in the moments you're meeting
Back out and just let them pass by.

1810.
Your joy and your sorrow can stand side-by-side,
For the two are quite different things:
Your joy is a constant that wells from inside
While your sorrow's what living life brings.

Emotions will come and emotions will go,
You can cling or allow them to pass,
But the clinging will quite often cause them to grow
Till they make of your mind a morass.

1811.
There are no limits that lessen your soul;
No bounds to what you can become,
But when you make gathering goods be your goal
And start seeing yourself as the sum

Of all of the things that you claim as your own,
You are building a prison of pride,
So step out of that cell where you languish alone
And cast all that you carry aside.

1812.
Sin applies salt to the soil of the soul
As it poisons the deep well of wisdom,
But love purifies, and makes healthy and whole
The lost spirit that longs for its freedom.

1813.
Step one is to dehumanize,
And make them less than you,
To justify and minimize
The things you plan to do.

Step two is cover up your tracks
Before you've laid them down,
So any trails that tie the acts
To you cannot be found.

Step three is to convince your mind,
For one last time, you're right.
Step four you move ahead and find
You've lost your precious light.

1814.
Abandon all things you believe to be true,
And search for the beacon of being,
That shines with a loving light deep inside you
And reflects off of all you are seeing.

Just loosen the layers that lessen that light,
And let it shine out unobstructed,
Then watch it illuminate, brilliant and bright,
The facade that our culture's constructed.

1815.
You've always had, deep down within,
A bright, unbounded beauty;
A lovely light that's yours and yours alone,

And all along it's always been
Your destiny and duty,
To live your life such that your soul is shown.

So shine it out unceasingly
And share in celebration,
With others, all the joy I'm speaking of,

That they can see with clarity

From your illumination
With clear, white light of luminescent love.

1816.
How does the end of winter make me feel?
Like letting out a breath long held inside,
Like harking to a church bell's distant peal,
Like knowing one more year I haven't died.

But also like I'll miss the falling snow
And water rushing neath the icy shell,
That clings to banks where when it's warm I'll go,
And long for when I hear that distant bell.

1817.
Morning and coffee and slow, gentle waking
While shedding the dross of a dream,
I see the self meld with this mind of my making
Until the two seamlessly seem

To be the same thing, but they're not and I know it;
I'm more than these thoughts in my head
That boil up and bolt from my brain like a bullet,
For I'm that which hears what is said.

1818.
We each have a hankering hunger inside
That we think we can quell with consumption,
Till our wallets grow thin and our hips become wide
And we find that a faulty assumption.

For what we are yearning for cannot be bought
And the hunger will always be there,
So it's only by turning away from what's taught,

And by being awake and aware,

That we'll learn to let go of the cravings that come
And not cling to them as they pass by,
And discover that happiness isn't the sum
Of the things that they taught us to buy.

1819.
What is the soul, is it only a dream;
Just a story we tell to stay sane?
Is it really no more than a well meaning meme
That we all pass along brain to brain?

I cannot say why but I feel in my heart
That there lies at the root of what's real,
A something (a soul?) that's my most precious part
And gives life to these feelings I feel.

1820.
The first thing I remember
Was waking in my bed,
To see the world in crystal clarity,

The day that tiny ember
Of consciousness was fed
With spirit to ignite the light in me.

1821.
Life's moments are such sacred things
That can be seen as such
By seeking out the light each brings
And tuning to the touch,

Of loving luminosity

That flows out of that glow,
So wake, that you might come to see
The truth you yearn to know.

1822.
When you deconstruct yourself
Down to the very core,
You'll find that what you thought was self
Is really self no more,

But is a fleeting false facade
You put on to appease
Society which, as your god,
You try so hard to please.

1823.
You'll never really know what you desire
Till you release your grip on what is near,
And set your sights on seeking something higher
Than all the things you waste your time on here.

And when attained, that life of nagging need,
In retrospect, will seem like nothing more
Than petty goals of avarice and greed,
That never came to make your spirit soar.

1824.
Step back from all your moments
And see them from afar,
Far from the flesh which foments
The inner waves of war,

Which drag you in and under,
While gasping for a breath;

Step back and wake with wonder,
Far beyond the bounds of death.

1825.
May your day be magical,
With all your moments merry;
May it become a hymn of harmony

With nature, long and lyrical;
A song whose callings carry
Across the high hills of humanity.

1826.
Do you believe you're somehow blessed
With self-awareness while the rest
Of life knows nothing close to consciousness?

That man alone can think and feel
While other creatures have no real
Experience of loss or happiness?

For ages we lived side-by-side
As equal beings, satisfied
With living out the little lives we led,

But now we're cruel beyond belief
And give the rest of nature grief;
How wicked are these ways to which we're wed.

1827.
We live within a world which we've
Imagined into being,
Yet we believe these fictions to be real.

So fully do these tales deceive
That we've begun agreeing
That truth is found in that which they reveal.

But all these stories we create
Are that, and nothing more;
Just tales we tell that we might all agree,

To fix a framework to our fate
We think's worth fighting for,
While all, in fact, remains a mystery.

1828.
Your suffering arises from inside you,
When you cling to the things that you desire,
And burns you so, for every time you've tried to
Put out the blaze it only stoked the fire.

But that's because, by actively engaging,
Though only doing so to gain release,
Your mind becomes attached to what you're craving,
With hungering that never seems to cease.

But if you stand aside and let the yearning
Pass by while you observe it come and go,
You'll find the burning hunger slowly turning
Into the perfect peace you long to know.

1829.
Get out of your head and discover what's real
When the thick clouds of thought clear away,
Or stay till you're dead and miss out on the feel
Of untethering from what they say.

For you're not the thoughts, but the one who's aware

Of the thoughts as they come and they go,
That will tie you in knots if you cling to them there,
Or will teach you what you need to know.

1830.
That person over there I see
Is labeled by society,
And is to it expected to conform,

But labels are just words that we
Apply to things we want to be
In line with what we think to be the norm.

1831.
What value are you to the system you serve,
And what then when that value is gone?
Are you but a twinge of its tiniest nerve;
Just a move of its paltriest pawn?

Will you grovel and grope to get back in the fold?
Will you be what it wants you to be?
Will you buy into all of the lies you've been told,
Or stand up for the right to be free?

1832.
The time has come for choosing
Just who it is you are,
For far too long you've failed to take a stand,

So shed your fear of losing
What you have gained so far;
Don't worry no one else will understand.

1833.
A part of us can touch and feel
The world in which we live,
And there's a part that makes sense of it all,

And where the two combine our real
Awareness grows to give
Life meaning as we hearken to its call.

1834.
We can let technology, which is our tool today,
Consume us till it has the upper hand,
Or we could throw reliance on technology away,
And once again live solely off the land.

Or maybe find some middle ground where we retain control,
And data lives to serve society;
Where it exists to sanctify each solitary soul
And be the handmaid of humanity.

1835.
What evil lies behind those eyes
That look back into mine?
What wily wicked wildness waits within?

I think you tame, but know you came
Out of a feral line
That would have stalked and savaged me back then.

1836.
Stop the music if it doesn't move you,
And from the silence seek a simple song,
Then tune it till the rhythm of it rings true,
For you're the judge of what is right and wrong.

1837.
With one foot in chaos and one amid order,
You'll walk the fine line of the Way,
And what you will find as you straddle that border
Will carry you throughout the day,

For by anchoring into the bedrock of Being,
While leaving the anchor line long,
You can visit the far-away lands you are seeing,
Then come home to where you belong.

1838.
Cast order into chaos if it binds you,
And see what rises up to take its place,
Lest you become complacent when it blinds you
By holding up a farce before your face.

For we are far too often fine with doing,
For comfort, what society demands,
When we should all be purposely pursuing
New paths and patterns in these shifting sands.

1839.
We are again a world at war;
What cost will it incur?
Will echoes of it travel far;
Will scars of it endure?

I fear, not for the damage or
The money it will cost,
But for the innocent and for
The lives they will have lost.

1840.
Putin's actions were inane
When he sent troops into Ukraine;
The fumbling of a fool about to fall,

For there was nothing there to gain
But scorn and an enduring stain
Upon the Russian people, one and all.

1841.
There is a sense of certainty
Within a winter day;
A solemn state suffusing all I see,

As in the stillness of a tree,
All barren, bleak and gray,
That waits with such potentiality.

1842.
Do you fear irrelevance;
That you might matter not?
That what you've taken as your stance
Just doesn't mean a lot?

Or are the things that you believe
Believed so through and through,
That you don't care what they perceive
Who judge the things you do?

1843.
With the sun in my face and a full day ahead,
I walk through this wakening wood,
In search of a sign or a signal to steady my soul.

For in nature the best of my being is bred
And, bonded with all that is good,
Becomes, in the harmony, healthy and happy and whole.

1844.
If I had only known, back then,
That nothing can be known,
I would have been more open to what's new,

But I'll not be that way again,
Now that the seed is sown,
That every day sets yesterday askew.

1845.
Who'll speak up for the ordinary person,
Who simply tries to make it through the day,
While all the world does all it can to worsen
Their life by taking all it can away.

It seems that we have lost the craft of caring
For others in the way we used to do,
And focus on ourselves instead of sharing
Our vast resources with the ones with few.

1846.
If I had only known back then
What's on my mind today,
I would have lived a different life indeed,

But who's to say it would have been
Improved in any way,
For maybe I'd have withered like a weed?

1847.
Sometimes I feel there is a veil,
Upon which is projected,
A vision of this wondrous world we see,

And all that's real, has its detail
Distorted when reflected
Off of that veil as our reality.

If you should peek, from your desire,
To see behind the curtain,
You may find you can never turn away,

For what you seek, that cleansing fire
Of truth, will show for certain
The land where loving luminescence lay.

1848.
Value the organic,
Though digital will do
You well in certain instances, but data isn't you,

It's purely algorithmic,
And only flesh can feel,
So live within your body now and revel in what's real.

1849.
The words that you say, they mean nothing to me,
They're just noises I choose to ignore,
For they're only cliches spoken repeatedly
And too often I've heard them before.

If there is a thing that you want to convey
I will hear, if it comes from the heart,
But if not, my attention will soon drift away

So you're best not to bother to start.

1850.
There is a thing I've never felt,
And will but only once,
When I at last depart my dying day,

As all my senses slowly melt
To insignificance,
And self-awareness simply drifts away.

1851.
It is the times of suffering and sorrow,
That makes the pleasant moments so profound,
For no one knows which one will come tomorrow,
But when it's good we revel all around.

How dull it all would be if all were perfect,
And everything was always without flaw,
For from the dissonance there comes the affect
We feel within as wonderment and awe.

1852.
I think the time has come at last
To move against the upper caste;
To sink their ships and burn their mansions down.

For with the wealth of one percent
Upon the poor, downtrodden spent,
They'll rise as opportunities abound.

1853
We are so totally consumed

With taking data in,
That I'm afraid we'll all be doomed
Unless we soon begin

To see that we're too tightly bound
To this technology,
And shed the web in which we're wound
While we can still break free.

1854.
I love a March snow
When the grass has gone green
And stands up through a wonder of white,

For at such times I know
That just knowing I've seen
A small wonder makes all the world right.

1855.
I looked up from my phone to see
I sat amid a crowd
(So lost was I within the web a while),

And marveled at the fact that we,
Though one, are each endowed
With differences we somehow reconcile.

1856.
We live for a while in a window of wealth
Where we feel we are healthy and whole,
While forgetting the masses who haven't our health
And who take every day a tall toll

Upon their whole being from every side,

And who struggle each day to survive.
Oh my God how we puff up with self-centered pride,
While the poor remain barely alive.

1857.
I stand on the beach and look out on the sea,
And I wonder how far I could swim,
Before I would be out so far out of reach
That my chance of survival was slim.

Just what would I find if I cast all aside
And took out to the sea straight away?
Would I find in the surf and the sea and the tide
What I seek nearly every day?

1858.
The sea, the surf, the sun, the sky,
It all so quickly passes by,
Until the beach is just a memory

Of sand that shifts beneath the feet,
Of sun, with its relaxing heat,
Of waking in a chair beside the sea.

1859.
A rich and verdant forest floor,
A meadow damp with dew,
The cool quiescence of a quiet stream.

The smell of rain evokes much more
Than I can tell to you,
For always it comes drifting like a dream.

1860.
Seek joy in everything you do,
Lest woe comes creeping in
To fill that place of emptiness inside,

For what you seek will come to you,
If you would but begin
To make pursuit of happiness your guide.

1861.
The bones beneath that weathered stone
Lie still as still can be,
But once they bore a body just like mine,

And someone knew it as their own
And longed, like you and me,
To light the lamp of love and let it shine.

1862.
I love the gentle hiss of cane
That dances in the breeze,
Its soft and soulful singing soothes me so,

Like sleeping through a night of rain,
Like surf and sun and seas,
Whose sanguine songs each serenade me slow.

1863.
So there you are, the pinnacle of all, or so you think,
So far above the rest of life is man.
So there it is, the sacred sect you feel provides the link
Between your god and people in his plan.

So there you stand, a citizen of the society

That is, in all ways, better than the rest,
But all I see that's great is your thick veil of vanity,
To which your selfish actions all attest.

You're but a child that deals with, every day, a dogged doubt,
And feels inside a constant, nagging need
To answer all the questions that your worry is about,
And not just live, but constantly succeed.

For you've been taught that winning over others is the way
To not fall, in your failure, far behind,
But could it be that living, simply living, every day
Would bring what, in all that, you hope to find?

1864.
The thing I'd like the sea to know
Above all else is this,
That in its waves that come and go
I find unbounded bliss.

They raise me up and let me down,
Then raise me up again,
And sing to me the soothing sound
Of water, waves and wind.

1865.
What does it take to be happy inside;
To feel joy at the seat of your soul?
It takes setting the things that you cling to aside
And becoming, through emptiness, whole.

But how do you empty what longs to be full?
You perceive that it really does not;
That it's only the powerful, persistent pull
Of the teachings that you have been taught.

1866.
You need to know yourself, and soon,
Before technology
Knows you so well it claims you for its own,

For each day you march to its tune
And follow mindlessly,
It's orders, with your face down in your phone.

1867.
What if there is no meaning;
No purpose to it all?
What if there is no Heaven
And no Hell to which to fall?

Where would you then be leaning;
What path would you pursue,
To be the moral leaven
Permeating all you do?

1868.
If I could I'd say to Christ
"If you could speak today,
What words would turn this fractured world around?",

And he'd respond, "With this zeitgeist,
There's nothing much to say,
Since all appears to be to badness bound".

1869.
Question everything you know
Until there's nothing left
That doesn't have a modicum of doubt,

And you will soon see answers grow,
Out of a life bereft
Of meaning, which show what your life's about.

1870.
Don't search for ancient answers
To what confronts you now,
For what you'll find will lead your life astray,

Instead, take tiny tinctures
Of truth, to show you how
To live, out of the teachings of today.

1871.
You know so very little of it all,
And what you know is hard to understand,
But don't despair that what you know is small,
Rejoice, instead, that what you know is grand.

When I was young I climbed to tops of trees,
And there encountered whispers in the wind,
But every time I reached my hand to seize
The truth, I'd slip and have to climb again.

Your knowing comes, not from the drawing in
And holding tightly to the things you find,
But from release and letting go your yen
For holding them forever in your mind.

So seek the wisdom in the here and now,
Then let it go and seek it out some more,
For only then will you discover how
To find the truth that you've been searching for.

1872.
My soul, like the sun, shines the same every day,
But my heart, like the moon, comes and goes,
And my sun and my moon see each other this way:
As two irreconcilable foes.

For my sun abhors shadows and drives them away,
While my moon does a dance in the dark,
But the two, when tied tightly together this way
Come to strike a most magical spark.

1873.
Don't stay in a world where you wallow in woe
When there are so many more places to go;
Don't sit there in sorrow and limit the life that you lead.

Instead, step away and start looking for more,
To find what awaits you beyond the next door,
For it's up to you to determine how you will proceed.

1874.
There is a force, like gravity,
That drags the spirit down,
But only when you cling to its embrace,

For you have the capacity
To turn yourself around,
By letting go and giving in to grace.

1875.
I fret about the future;
There's few of us who do,
Too few to alter what's about to be,

For it is in our nature
To talk, but not pursue,
When change affects us individually.

Our hope's in adolescents,
Who have the most to lose,
And need to start a revolution now,

To put down, with their presence,
And with the lives they choose,
The god of growth to which their parents bow.

For they can see what's noble
(With clear and youthful eyes,
And minds unclouded by hypocrisy)

Are gains whose goals are global,
For which, as one, they'll rise,
Above the needs of nationality.

1876.
There is no path or practice,
No peak you must pursue,
No guru to apprentice
Who will show the way to you.

For what you seek is lying,
Right there before your eyes,
So take it and stop trying
To find truth where little lies.

1877.
It's easy to get lost within
The mind of the collective,
And act in ways that later you'll regret,

For mass appeal has often been
A poisonous perspective,
That seems so right when people follow it.

Before you choose to join a thing
Discover its objective,
To find out what it's going to ask of you,

And if it doesn't have the ring
Of truth, then irrespective
Of what it takes, avoid what isn't true.

1878.
When someone tries to reach me,
And yet I miss their call,
I feel as though I've failed them in this way:

That they called to beseech me,
To save them from a fall,
And that they fell because I was away.

1879.
Speak against the act and not the actor;
It's not for you to judge or to condemn.
Instead of speaking out as an accuser,
Show, by your ways, a better path to them.

For you will not convince through accusation,
Someone that they should take a different course,
But by example and by reputation,
You can become, for them, a saving source.

1880.
My muse was talking all night long;

Just rambling on and on,
With words that echoed back to where they started,

Until I heard a quiet song
That sang about the dawn,
And as it rose insomnia departed.

1881.
I watch a thin cloud
Roll in from the west,
First amber, then bright to rust red,

Like life, that's endowed
With change that won't rest,
And permanence never quite shed.

1882.
There is, in life, a reason and a rhythm,
A purpose and a wave on which it rides,
That springs from an eternal algorithm
That, based on input, mindlessly decides.

But we decide the input to provide it,
By what we do along this life we lead,
Such that the world we know which comes out of it
Is totally dependent on each deed.

1883.
Do not pretend to be a thing
You know that you are not,
And find one day your life is but a lie,

For living out the truth will bring
The ends you've always sought,

Which you will find have always been nearby.

1884.
The world is alive with blossoming beauty
Reborn in the sprouting of spring,
To color the woods and soften the city,
And open their petals to sing

A sweet song of hope, and growth and becoming,
As they turn to soak in the sun,
While I walk these woods which wake to the warming,
Delighted the blooming's begun.

1885.
We all can smell the dank decay
Of death and deep decline,
And yet we live from day to day
Like everything is fine,

Pretending that the world is well
And will forever be,
While all the while the solemn knell
Portends catastrophe.

We came into a paradise
Where all was lush and green,
But living thus did not suffice
To quell our hungering,

For every time we saw excess
We greedily consumed,
And tamed the wider wilderness
Which steadily succumbed

To pressure till there was no ground

We hadn't stepped upon,
And we'd consumed all that we found
Till all was nearly gone.

But we still have a chance, I think,
To turn it all around,
Before we step across the brink,
To loose what we have bound,

And work for the eternity
That was and still could be,
Where Earth, in her fertility,
Is home for you and me.

1886.
It's a slippery slope
From the highlands of hope
To the desert of death and despair,

And it takes but a day
To slide down all the way
When your life takes a turn you can't bear,

But there's nothing to stop
Your way back to the top,
Where belief, like a beacon, burns bright,

So rise up, if you will,
And climb back up that hill
To be one, once again, with the light.

1887.
You live your life until one day
You turn and look upon the way
You came, now in the past, forever gone,

And wonder how life moved so fast
And pine for pleasures of the past,
Then if you're wise, you'll turn and carry on.

1888.
Don't pity the poor for lacking the treasures
You cling to with such high regard,
For they can get by without all your pleasures;
What they lack makes living life hard.

For they lack the basics, like food on the table
And minimal medical care,
So pity the poor, that we are unable
To, from our self-centeredness, share.

1889.
What matters is right here and here alone,
Don't waste your time on dreams you'll never know,
Awaken to the world and you'll be shown
How from the simple things great treasures grow.

For instance, one small leaf seems most mundane,
Just one among a million in the wood,
And yet a wonder born of earth and rain;
The gift it gives is oft misunderstood.

In such a way is every blade of grass,
And every cloud that drifts across the sky,
So peer upon each person that you pass,
To meet the mote of magic in their eye.

1890.
I saw an old man while walking today,
Out working a while in his yard.

He told me his wife had long passed away,
And life has grown heavy and hard,

And yet he got out to tend to the beds
She'd planted, lest they too succumb,
In hope that the bulbs of yellows and reds
She loved so would once again bloom.

1891.
You are the one who listens,
So silently within,
You're not the voice which rattles on
With never-ending din.

You are the soul eternal
That's here but for a while,
To give to everyone you meet
The solace of a smile.

1892.
Lovely, that last little light that lingers,
When day has given over to the night,
As branches sway to wind that barely whispers
Through which the first few stars shine clear and bright.

Marvelous the moon that rises slowly,
That opalescent orb of lovely light,
Which weaves itself into the dark to show me
The path to take to navigate the night.

1893.
I yearned to find the weaver of this web
To which we are so very tightly bound,
And see what drives its constant flow and ebb,

But in the act of seeking I have found

That answers are obscured when asking why,
So I abandoned that investigation,
And when I did, the fog was lifted by
The wind of wisdom in that realization.

1894.
I look with awe upon each thing
As it emerges in the spring,
Though I have seen them many times before,

And think, what other buds of bliss
And magic moments do I miss
That I have seen, and seeing once ignore.

1895.
When I am old and worthless
Don't put me in a home,
I'd rather you release me in the wild.

And don't think cold and helpless,
In deep despair I'd roam,
For in the woods I'd be again a child.

There I'd be hale and happy,
And live off of the land,
And revel in my struggle to survive.

But you'll want what's best for me,
And never understand
That cared for I'd be only half alive.

1896.
You feel what you feel
And those feelings are real,
They are yours, and they're in your control.

You know what you know
And your knowledge can grow
If you focus your mind on your goal.

You love what you love
And you hate what you hate,
As you move through the world you're amid,

And you die when you die
And you'll never know why
Your life followed the path that it did.

1897.
What emerges from the whole,
As each of us is thinking,
And sharing, with each other, what we find,

Becomes for us a common goal
Enlivened by the linking
Of threads of thought arising from each mind.

1898.
Just think of how we have evolved
To what we are today,
From what, so very long ago, we were,

And how, so steadily, we solved
The obstacles that they
Who came before our time, had to endure.

Though we have changed we have retained
Thin traces of the past
That show themselves in who we are today,

As echoes of what has remained
And will forever last,
While much of what we're now will pass away.

1899.
The difficult things that are hard to accept
Are the easiest things to ignore.
At doing that we are all very adept;
We are masters at closing that door.

But acting as though life contains only good
Will not lead to escape from what's bad,
So turn to and mourn for the things that you should,
Lest you look back and wish that you had.

1900.
I walk through the woods and it's there that I find
An escape for a moment from what's in my mind;
An escape and a bonding again with a world that is real.

For these lives that we lead can be hard on the soul,
And it's hard to let go and be once again whole,
But I've found when I do it is then that I truly can feel.

1901.
Each of us is taught to binge
Upon the middle ground,
But it is out there on the fringe
That flavor can be found,

So take a risk and let your mind
Explore where you've not been,
And you'll be freed by what you find
To take a risk again.

1902.
Now that I'm near the end I see
That it is still a mystery,
And that I found no answer to it all,

And yet I know with certainty
That that was not the goal; that the
Whole purpose was to consummate the call.

And what was I called to pursue?
What task was I supposed to do?
What was the reason for my being here?

It was, I think to live and love,
And spread about the goodness of
The world that was awaiting, oh so near.

1903.
Learning is not about taking in facts
And echoing what you've been told.
Those mostly are mindless and meaningless acts,
To you, from society, sold.

Learning is all about opening eyes
And finding one's way in the world,
And slowly becoming, all by yourself, wise
As all the real facts are unfurled.

1904.
Love is a stream that wells up from within
And flows forth like a spring on a mountain,
That spills down and waters the meadows below
As a gift from that fast flowing fountain.

For love leads to life, and it always has been
The sole source of our strength and salvation,
So let your love join with and follow the flow
That comes constantly out of creation.

1905.
You're the love of my life,
You're my one and my all,
You're the reason I rise from my bed.

You're my strength when there's strife
And a hand when I fall;
I'm so glad you're the one that I wed.

1906.
We each have the choice
To be the lone voice
And to call out when things are not right,

Or conform to the crowd;
So compelling and loud.
When it's wrong will you stand up and fight?

1907.
You've always been in motion and emergent,
And always in a state of soon to be,
Each day you rise as newly formed and nascent,
Each night you dream of what you soon will see.

But if one day you think you're done evolving,
And that there will be always nothing new,
Know that the hands of change are still revolving,
And always will within the heart of you.

1908.
One day you'll find your true love gone,
And yet you'll hear the birds chirp on
As you awake alone there in your bed,

But you'll find strength to carry on,
And rise to look upon the dawn,
By reminiscing in the morning red.

1909.
Those who will not compromise,
They do not understand
The nature of a true democracy,

Whose purpose is to slowly rise
Above each selfish stand;
Their stubbornness is but hypocrisy.

1910.
Who are we as a nation
If we do not place above
The right to arm, the safety of a child?

It is an indication
Of a selfish lack of love
In those who claim they can't be reconciled.

1911.
We live in the moment, the here and the now;
The past is a far-away fiction;
The future no more than the dim shifting shades of a dream.

Yet we pine for those things, unaware of just how,
If we're mindful of every action,
We'll find what we seek, for these moments are more than they
seem.

1912.
Oh how I love the silhouette
Of trees against the sky
When evening comes to take the light away.

From when the sinking sun has set
Till stars shine from on high,
It is a contemplative time of day.

1913.
We read a wealth of meaning
Into that which is mundane,
And therein lies the magic of the mind,

For it is always leaning
In to posit and explain
The purpose of each fleeting form we find.

1914.
Be always ready to receive
The wisdom from within,
That comes upon you as epiphany,

To test the truths that you believe,

And that have always been
The cornerstones of your reality.

1915.
There is a light that lies within
And shines, at times without;
A gentle light, like that which brings the dawn

Out of the quiet darkness when
The stars are all about.
Who will you choose to shine your light upon?

1916.
What serves, for you, as verity,
What is your source of truth?
What stones are your foundation built upon?

Do you still follow desperately
Your paradigms of youth,
Now that the world you knew so well is gone?

1917.
You roll with it all, yes you do, yes you do,
You roll with it all don't you know it,
And you'd probably change but a bit of it all
If you had half a chance to redo it.

You're born and you die and it's all up to you
To find you a path worth your walking;
To pursue what is true and to follow the call,
And to do more than dreaming and talking.

You roll with it all, yes you do, yes you do,
You roll like a stone on a mountain;

Like a stream tumbling down, crystal clear, cold and true,
Flowing forth from a fast flowing fountain.

You live and you love and each moment is new;
Each day brings its toll and its treasure,
And it's nobody else's but yours to pursue,
So seek in it your passion and pleasure.

1918.
Sometimes a gloom gets in my head,
That dims the living light
Such that I cannot see beyond the day,

And miss the joys that lie ahead,
So stifled is my sight,
Until they come and wash my woes away.

1919.
She covers her tracks when her stream pulls you in
And tucks you up under a bank,
To wrap you in roots till you are but a bundle of bones.

She's done it before and she'll do it again;
Suck down every soul that has sank.
This river is greedy and all who slip under she owns.

1920.
Let's walk together, you and I,
Ere time splits us asunder,
To see what things we two can spy,
And marvel at the wonder

Of all the magic mystery
We come across while walking,

And share together what we see
Without a bit of talking.

We'll come across a flowing creek
And wade out in the quiet,
And as we turn each rock we'll seek
The life that lies below it.

We'll walk into a meadow bright
And feel the sun upon us,
And bathed in its life-giving light
We'll revel in its warmness,

Then cool off in a quiet grove
Where sunbeams search the shadows,
While we, enraptured by them, rove
In search of ghostly grottoes.

Let's walk together, you and I,
Let's walk along together,
For soon this life will pass us by
And we'll be gone forever.

1921.
The moon, a star, a lightning bug,
The singing of the night,
The cricket creak of slowly passing time.

The drifting off, then gentle tug
Awake to morning light;
So simple, yet so soulfully sublime.

1922.
With feet propped up and hat pulled low
I drift into a dream,

While serenaded by the summer sounds,

And drink it up because I know,
Though summertime may seem
A time of endless days, it has its bounds.

1923.
Sometimes you're touched by tongues of fire,
Sometimes your fields lie fallow,
Sometimes your soul sings like a choir,
Sometimes its song seems shallow.

Yet you ride out the waves of woe
With faith in what's to follow,
For you have seen them come and go
And know their haunts are hollow.

1924.
When at last you're dead and gone
Will someone pass your memory on,
To grant, through memory, immortality?

Or will your life, once dead and cold,
Be deemed not worthy to be told?
Will you epitomize ignominy?

1925.
We seek the truth in all we see,
We yearn to know the answers,
For we desire conformity,
With all in step, like dancers.

With all in step and moving to
The music of the maker;

With all forever acting through
The giver and the taker.

The giver when it's going good,
The taker when it's not;
The architect who's understood
As building what we've got.

We seek a single source from where
All order emanates,
But could it be this whole affair
Is formed of fortune's fates?

1926.
I have inside a hunger,
A burning, raw desire,
That's raged, since I was younger,
As an unrelenting fire,

That's been a constant yearning,
A nagging nascent need,
That drives me to discerning
What is deep in every deed.

1927.
There is no reason to arise;
Sleep in, the rain is falling.
Sleep in and let it take you far away.

Just snuggle in and close your eyes
And listen to its calling,
And let it's drifting dream decide your day.

1928.
These are the moments you live for,
These moments of magic and mirth,
These days of delight that you'd die for,
And sought since the day of your birth.

It's not the long length of your living,
Or that which you gain on the way,
But finding the gifts life is giving
And gifting them back every day.

1929.
I saw a yellow woolly worm
A waving down the trail,
I paused my pace a bit that it not die.

It might be accident or germ
That makes your life to fail;
Will fate adjust its step when it comes by?

1930.
I will slip into a sleep,
An endless slumber, dark and deep,
When death comes gently knocking at my door.

Will I wake on some other side
Or be reborn, once I have died,
Or will I simply be around no more?

1931.
There it is, mortality.
No, wait, don't look away!
Ignoring it won't change a single thing,

For you will die eventually;
It simply works that way.
Accept it like all else your life will bring.

1932.
I promise you the world, my love,
Though that seems far away,
And all I have right now is what you see,

Yet you and I will rise above,
The limits of today,
For love will take us where we long to be.

1933.
You think you've got it figured out
And know the world so well,
But yours is but a fleeting fantasy,

And you'd best learn what it's about
Before your final bell,
Lest you find that you've missed reality.

1934.
The song of self is sung in you,
In you and you alone;
It tells a tale that never has been told,

Of what you've done and hope to do,
And wonders you've been shown;
A song that sings the happiness you hold.

1935.
We are not the flesh we feel,

Though that is all we know
And have been told that there is nothing more,

For from the root of what is real
Strong streams of spirit flow,
Through which we're each connected to the core.

1936.
There's a breeze that always blows
And carries us along,
There's a tune the spirit knows
That is our soulful song,

There's a movement in the mind
Discerning what is real,
But in the heart is where you'll find
The truth in how you feel.

1937.
It's okay to not agree,
In fact that's how it's meant to be,
It's normal you'll not always get your way.

But in the end there will be found,
Between you two, some common ground,
If you'd but seek some truth in what they say.

1938.
Where has the common struggle gone
That made us work as one?
Where is the stream that pulled us all along?

It seems we've all been stranded on
The route we used to run;

It seems we've lost the substance of our song.

1939.
What kind of world would you prefer to see,
One filled with kindness or hostility?
What kind of life would you prefer to live,
One of revenge or one where you forgive?

It's up to us to make a paradise
Or let it spiral down to mean from nice,
We only need to key on being kind
And tolerate the differences we find.

1940.
Come to me, oh muse of mine,
Come to me if you will,
With words that weave a tapestry to tell,

And I will write them, line by line,
As from my heart they spill,
Like water overflowing from a well.

1941.
I'm seeking a simplicity
That's here but hard to hold,
And has within it all I need to know,

But lost in the complexity
I hardly can behold
The thing I seek, so little does it show.

Like hearing, in cacophony,
The singing of the soul;
Like ascertaining truth amid the lies,

The seeing of simplicity
Means looking at the whole,
And looking through it all with watchful eyes.

1942.
There is, of course, no certainty,
All can be falsified,
Yet from experience we build belief,

And from belief, dependency
On what is quantified,
But what we know is transient and brief.

1943.
Is there a cloud of dark despair
That hovers over you?
Do you live in a pointless pit of pain?

Don't wait there till the loving care
Of helping hands come through,
For you might find your waiting is in vain.

Your destiny is up to you,
Your future's in your hands,
Your path ahead is paved by you alone,

And all depends on what you do
When met with life's demands,
And how you feel when facing the unknown.

1944.
That tree over there moves in myriad ways,
Its leaves like a flock of black birds,
Its rippling form silhouetted against the late sky,

Like the shadows of thought that we see through the haze,
Which we work at to weave into words,
Yet never are sure of the truth of the terms we apply.

1945.
It has been, throughout history,
Our nagging need to know
The truth that's moved society ahead;

To turn and face uncertainty
And learn, when doing so,
A thing or two about ourselves instead.

1946.
How can this deep experience
Of being who we are
Arise out of mere matter to be mind?

And yet, somehow we all can sense
Ourselves from what's afar;
Between the two a boundary's defined.

If self-awareness can arise
From matter on its own,
It must arise the same in other kinds,

And consciousness, we must surmise,
Would certainly have grown
Into the sentience of other minds.

1947.
Emerging from the long-forgotten root,
There will, one day, arise a single shoot,
And from that shoot the tree of life will grow.

And from that tree the fruit to feed us all,
And from the fruit the strength to hear the call,
And from the call, the news we need to know.

1948.
Your days roll by like tumbleweeds,
Your nights, they come and go,
And one day you'll awake to find them gone.

So grasp, before the chance recedes,
Your life, that you might know
The purpose of the path that you are on.

1949.
It's the hush of the woods in the morning,
And the brush of the breeze through the branches,
That draws me out into the forest to take in the air.

And the way, now and then, without warning,
A beam of light comes through and catches,
And holds my attention such that I just stand there and stare.

And what sights do I see in the shadows,
As the light plays and dances there dimly?
What moves me to stand there and stare out in wonder and awe?

My attention is captured by echoes
Of the past that comes flowing through faintly,
Then fade away fast before I can be sure what I saw.

1950.
Love is a hurt that just won't go away;
It's an aching down deep in your heart.
Hate is a demon that darkens your day;

It's a curtain that's closed and won't part.

Anger's a fire that burns out of control;
Fear is a weight that you wear,
And together they sculpt out the shape of your soul,
And the lay of the life that you share.

1951.
Look into a heart and you will find infinity;
There are no bounds to keep love from expanding.
Look into your own and it is likely you will see
You've missed that point from where you have been standing.

There's nothing in a heart but boundless love and energy;
There is no room for darkness or descending,
And if you'd shift your stance there is a possibility
This life you live might have a happy ending.

1952.
Immerse yourself deeply where nothing is known,
Down deep in the vast vacant void;
It's there you'll find treasures you never quite knew you desired,

For springing up out of the seeds you had sown
In the past, that you thought were destroyed,
There grows a great goodness, to which, long ago, you aspired.

1953.
Stepping back through many generations;
Back to the ancient times when life began,
We find a constant branching of relations
Out of the primal form of life to man.

But though it has branched out in all directions,

All life is still a single entity,
That's bound together by the vast connections
That ties each living thing to you and me.

1954.
There's no intentionality
That orchestrated all;
There is no architect or master plan,

For life acquired complexity
In changes very small,
Through random steps from single cell to man.

But still I feel there seems to be
A mover moving all,
That has a hand in how life is aligned,

And so I listen patiently
To hear its quiet call,
And see what words of wisdom I can find.

1955.
We love the use of labels to define identity
And specify the people that we are,
But when we cling too tightly to our nationality
We easily are herded into war.

It's hard, when we define ourselves, to let those labels go,
For often they're defined as all or none,
But when they change from good to bad we need to see them so,
And know our time to side with them is done.

1956.
Don't focus on the finding

Of a fallacy in faith,
That those who follow faith cannot defend,

For there need be no binding
Tween what ancient voices saith,
And that which scientific thought can lend.

1957.
Each of us live lives of many layers;
We're not the simple single selves we seem,
Like music that's composed for many players;
Like all the varied currents in a stream.

So do not think you know someone for certain,
For just as soon as you believe you do,
Your view of them will part just like a curtain,
And you will be exposed to something new.

1958.
Science and religion should seek out and embrace
Their overlapping commonality,
And where they're not in common, they need to know their place,
And thus support that deep diversity.

For one explores the outer, through objectivity,
By measuring and testing what is real;
The other delves the inner, through subjectivity,
Exploring who we are and how we feel.

1959.
Remember when it was okay
To simply not agree;
Back when we valued freedom of belief?

What made us as we are today
With such polarity?
Can we just pause and turn another leaf?

1960.
This world is rich with meaning,
Much more than you can know,
But it is not intrinsic;
We make it as we go.

It comes from the convening
Of hearts that beat as one,
Emerging from the magic
As this tapestry is spun.

1961.
There is no deep reality,
From which all things arise,
What is lies on the surface that you see,

Not deep within each entity,
There inexistence lies,
What's real is their relationality.

1962.
The setting sun comes through the trees
Like bright, but fading memories;
The clarity of evening song begins,

With birdsong piercing through the hush
As all falls quiet from the rush
While sharpened by an introspective lens.

1963.
And there it is, that moment
When the twilight slips away,
And all falls down into the dark of night,

To kill the constant cadence
And the drumming of the day,
While stars illuminate the land with light.

1964.
We are all composed of many layers,
Each stacked atop the others one by one,
With each one adding something to the whole;

A song of self performed by many players,
Each singing out until its part is done,
For there are many voices to the soul.

1965.
It is the vast complexities,
And endless possibilities,
Of interconnectivities
Of neurons in the brain,

That gives us each abilities,
If we would only seek to seize
Our great potentialities,
To boundlessly attain.

1966.
Could it be that our God is within us?
For in each an infinity lies,
And the spaces inside us combine in the lives that we share.

Could it be God is not far above us,
But looks out from the depths of our eyes?
Could it be we love God when we treat one another with care?

1967.
What living things, besides ourselves,
Know subjectivity?
What other forms live in an inner world?

Is it just us who deeply delves
Within that secret sea?
In us alone is consciousness unfurled?

1968.
All life depends on taking in
The world and then responding;
For us, like all that lives, that is a fact.

But tween the two we live within
Our minds where we are bonding
The world with thought to choose how to react.

We are aware that we're in there
Deciding what we're doing,
And know that others live within the mind,

And it's the willingness to share
Those inner worlds we're viewing
That gives our lives the meaning that we find.

1969.
Before I get much older,
Before the well runs dry,
Before a stillness settles on my soul,

Before my flesh grows colder,
Before the day I die,
I hope to know myself, and know it whole.

1970.
We all must follow something,
Some road of relevance,
And I believe without that we are lost,

But some paths lead to nothing
But blind obedience,
Where we incur an ever-rising cost.

The groups we join and follow
Are hard to leave behind,
When we've invested time and energy,

But when we find them shallow,
Or hateful or unkind,
We need to walk away and leave them be.

1971.
Before the Europeans came
In search of gold and freedom,
This land they saw as new was not at all,

For tribes too numerous to name,
Who knew no king or kingdom,
Had lived here long before the creeping sprawl

Of colonizing came to kill,
Through sickness and starvation,
Through dispossession and atrocity;

Through wrongs that were and happen still

Through misinterpretation
Of truth by our one-sided history.

1972.
No one knows how it would be
To be some other being;
We only know of being what we are.

No one knows what we would see
With other forms of seeing;
We only know that it would be bizarre.

No one knows how it would feel
To be a different form;
We only know the way we feel inside,

And that our sentience is real
And is, for us, the norm
We use when consciousness is codified.

1973.
Back then, way back before we knew
The nation we would turn into,
We saw ahead of us a rising sun,

That cast its light upon us all,
But politics has spread a pall
Upon the hopefulness of everyone.

For there is such polarity
And selfish spontaneity
That we no longer look for common ground,

But point a finger right away,
Which shows, in what we do and say,

Intolerance for differences found.

1974.
The day has passed into the night,
Its deeds have come and gone;
It's time to settle down into a sleep,

And all that's left that longs for light
Must wait until the dawn;
Must lay in wait through dreaming dark and deep.

1975.
I have in me immensity,
And it's the same for you,
And from it the propensity
To take a broader view,

But only when I look within,
Where lies infinity,
And see the world as but a skin
Atop reality.

1976.
We all are on a road that leads
To economic failure,
That's triggered by a great catastrophe,

And hear the siren that proceeds
The catastrophic closure
Of bridges back call to us frantically.

How can we stay upon this path
While knowing where it's leading?
How can we when we know what is to be?

How can we when the aftermath
Is towards us surely speeding?
We can because we all walk selfishly.

1977.
Why all this anger that we see
From those at the extremity
Who persecute in patriotic guise?

Why can't they all just get along,
And not see differences as wrong,
But that in tolerance our freedom lies?

1978.
I believe in miracles.
Do you believe it's true,
That scientific principles
Give way, at times, for you?

I believe the facts are strong,
And science is for real,
But also that it's often wrong;
I've faith in what I feel.

1979.
I'll take a sounding of my soul;
In dark deep depths, a trawling,
To see what I can pull up from below.

While waves upon the surface roll
And winds blow hard and howling,
The quiet depths sustain a steady flow.

And what I find is oftentimes

Not that which I was seeking;
Quite often I'm surprised at what is there,

When hints of what is real in rhymes,
Not of my mindful making,
Come rising from below for me to share.

1980.
Just what are the triggers that trip you,
Revising the rhythm you run?
What tempts you to turn, in a moment, away from your way?

Are you in control of what you do
Or under the thumb of someone
Who knows how to sway and oppress you and make you obey?

1981.
Seek that perfect point of peace
And settle there your soul,
Just settle like a stone into the sea,

Till dissonance has come to cease
And self is healed and whole,
And once again aligned in harmony.

Then let your peaceful spirit grow
And spread into the world,
To alter all it touches on the way,

And give off from it's gentle glow
The light of love unfurled,
To shine and shoo the shadows all away.

1982.
I seek the quietude of calmer waters,
Where I can find the stillness that I need
To set these stones before my tower totters,
And find my focus so I can proceed.

And what I seek, I know to be before me;
I know to be right here for me to find,
If I could only set my silent self free
From all this endless chatter of the mind.

1983.
I don't know who I'm praying to
Or what I hope to find,
I only know that when I go
Into my prayerful mind,

I lose the world and melt into
What seems a sacred place,
And in that temple come to know
Forever face-to-face.

1984.
Other minds, not ours alone,
Must know some sentience;
There must be other ways to be aware,

For other kinds of life have grown,
Through time, a cognizance
Of self, shown in behaviors that we share.

I feel there is a gradient
Where consciousness must grow
With gradually increasing sense of self,

As sensing of the salient
Externals slowly show
A living thing what's different from itself.

And as it does it formulates
A model held within,
And plays upon it what it aims to do,

And from that action contemplates
The way that what has been
Will change in time with that which will ensue.

So what does this tell to us of
The lives not like our own?
Should we assume all life's somewhat aware?

I think it says we need to love
All life, not man alone,
As if there were some sense of self in there.

1985.
There are no limits to our love,
No bounds to block our bliss,
Within our world there's only you and I,

As we together rise above
It all in happiness,
Like eagles soaring thermals in the sky.

1986.
I see you there, you're reading me
And wondering what to think;
That's something you must find all on your own,

For what I write's a mystery

Whose words are just a wink,
With meaning that you'll have to find alone.

1987.
You have in life one chance to find
Just who you are inside,
And when at last you free your mind
Your body will abide

With what you've found yourself to be,
Untethered from your shame,
And you, at last, will find you're free
To break from where you came.

1988.
As you encounter senescence
Your life will start to slow,
Just like a clock that only once is wound,

And when it does the radiance
Of youth will lose its glow,
But other gifts are waiting to be found.

For as you age you'll come to know
The sweetness of the soul,
That ripens on the fertile tree of time,

And feel the sea of stillness grow
Until you know it whole,
And slowly slip into that sea sublime.

1989.
What in this wondrous world sustains your soul?
What strengthens you and makes your spirit whole?

Or are you seeking something to provide
A food to fill the emptiness inside?

If so, you will not find it where you think,
If you think your possessions somehow link
You to the state of fullness you desire;
Seek nourishment instead in something higher.

1990.
Like a pebble made smooth in the bed of a stream,
My edges, once rough, are now rounded,
Like the phantoms that rise from the depth of a dream,
My worries, I've found, were unfounded.

Like the things I desired when I was a child,
There's much, I see now, that's not needed,
For time, that great arbiter, has reconciled
Where I was with the place my soul's seated.

1991.
The world that we're aware of,
And witness every day,
Is but a model held internally,

And is a partial view of
(Our Umwelt, you might say)
The full and unconstrained reality.

Our senses have developed
To take in what we need,
And leave the rest behind perception's door,

And so we have enveloped
A subset, and agreed
Among ourselves that there is nothing more.

But living here among us
Are creatures who perceive
Sensations we will never come to know,

So do not grow self righteous,
And try to not believe
That all that matters are the things that show.

1992.
What rises from our consciousness
Is relevance from randomness;
Is modeling the world in such a way,

That there's a structure on which we
Can build our own reality
That always stays the same from day to day.

For we take in the whole of it
Then filter out what doesn't fit
Within the form with which our world is cast,

But if with mindfulness you trace,
Before the filtering takes place,
The path of what you sense you'll see at last.

1993.
You build a model in your mind
Defining who you are,
Then one day wake and come to find
That your whole repertoire

Was built upon a sandy soil
That's washing all away,
And that your many years of toil
Were lost within a day.

But to tear down and build again
Is what you need to do;
To reassess who you have been
And build yourself anew,

For constantly the way you see
The world will rearrange,
And who you are will never be
Immutable to change.

1994.
You wake into the world one day,
Then find one day you're old;
You've changed, and yet the sky is just as blue.

And though your days have passed away,
The memories you hold
Will paint an evening sky of every hue.

1995.
We're all on the brink of disaster;
We're nearing the point where we'll find,
These changes that keep coming faster
Have left all our options behind.

But we have one moment remaining
To turn back this vessel we ride,
Before there is no more regaining;
Before our whole planet has died.

1996.
I love to get up early
And watch the day awake,
As colors grow and creep across the sky,

While slowly, very slowly,
I open up and take
It in before the morning passes by.

1997.
I think it's our children who'll save us,
From the fate to which we have been blind;
They'll do what is right and ignore us,
And act with the future in mind.

They'll see our short-sighted decisions
As self-centered stupidity,
And make every choice upon visions
Of preserving the earth and the sea.

1998.
It's easy for us not to see
The edges of society;
Those souls who suffer silently
From hunger and neglect.

It's easy for us to ignore,
When we don't live among the poor,
That what they really need is more
Of our sincere respect.

1999.
We are each a multitude,
And yet, expressed as one.
We are each an emptiness
Through which our souls are spun.

We are each a plentitude
Of personalities,

Of want and woe and happiness;
We're formed of all of these.

2000.
It isn't a matter of heaven or hell;
It's not if you win or you lose.
What matters is living, and living life well,
With great good in the choices you choose.

It's not about finding the answers to all,
Or gathering goods as you go,
What matters is caring when you hear the call
Of some person you don't even know.